MW00720885

The cover photo shows the entire student body and faculty of Woodman School near Lolo, Montana in 1903. The young man in the back row, left of the photo, was playfully hit on the head with a lunch pail by one of his classmates. He developed a large bruise, which a local doctor tried to lance with an unsterilized instrument. The boy developed an infection, which proved fatal. The teacher in the photo died of Rocky Mountain Spotted Fever a week after school was dismissed in the spring. The last surviving student in this photo passed away in the spring of 2003.

Leaving School: Finding Education

Jon Wiles
University of North Florida – Jacksonville

John Lundt
University of Montana – Missoula

Matanzas Press
St. Augustine, Florida

Library of Congress Cataloging-in-Publication Data

Wiles, Jon
           Leaving School: Finding Education / Jon Wiles, John Lundt
    Includes bibliographical references.
    1. Education reform – United States. 2. Schools – United States. I.
Wiles, Jon. II. Lundt, John. III. Title.
    Library of Congress Control Number 2003115977

This book has been produced electronically and without print dependence. The authors have written and exchanged ideas from three thousand miles distance. The book has been edited by Shannon McLeish of Ormond Beach, Florida. Composition and printing was completed by BookMasters in Mansfield, Ohio. No face-to-face contact took place as this book was assembled. Copies of this book may be purchased on-line from www.leavingschoolfindingeducation.com. For those still wary of all of these new things, orders can also be placed at Matanzas Press, 7840 Scenic Highway A1A, St. Augustine, Florida 32080.

The paper used in this publication meets the minimum requirements of the American National Standard for Information Sciences – Permanence of Paper for Printed Library Materials, ANSI Z39.48-1984.

ISBN: 0-9748731-0-1

About the Authors

Jon Wiles is a professor, author, and consultant specializing in curriculum change in schools. Dr. Wiles has written or co-authored more than a dozen texts in the area of educational leadership, and has worked as a consultant in over forty states and ten foreign nations. He presently serves as Professor of Education at the University of North Florida and as the President of Learningwebs, Inc., a non-profit corporation providing assistance to teachers in the development of Internet-based curriculum. Jon and his wife, Michele, reside in Crescent Beach, Florida.

John Lundt spent the first half of his career as a teacher and administrator in public secondary schools. For the past fifteen years he has served as Professor of Educational Leadership at the University of Montana where he teaches courses in curriculum leadership and futurism. As the founder and President of Educational Leadership Associates Inc., Dr. Lundt has consulted with educational agencies in Europe, Asia, and the Middle East as well as in Canada and the United States. John, his wife, Pamela, and their son, Jonathan, reside in Missoula, Montana.

Table of Contents

Preface

A tour of a school building leaves any visitor with the good feelings of hope and renewal. For here, assembled in this place called school, is our future. The laughing, smiling faces of the children, as well as the general familiarity of the place to all of us, dashes any hope of being objective in trying to understand this institution. In fact, only when you see all of those inquisitive young minds locked down on a single page, or hear one thousand voices silenced by an adult command, do you approach a true understanding of "school." Yes, school is a learning place, but the school demands compliance and conformity. The school dictates "what is" and defines what counts as learning.

The school is an arbitrary and often capricious mentor indeed. This stern and unbending institution may have been appropriate as a learning medium when education consisted of simple communication between a knowing teacher and an unknowing pupil. But this same institution, in the information-rich 21st century, is now deadly as a primary source of knowing. Schools are increasingly unfit to educate young persons who possess extensive prior knowledge, have access to new knowledge, and demonstrate a natural curiosity for learning. As a society, we now possess the tools to move forward, to leave the school behind, and to rediscover education. The time is right for America to disassemble our schools and to construct a new learning medium for our children.

We begin this book by exploring the fragile state of schooling in America, and then proceed to follow the decline of our schools up to the present. We will liken schools to other major institutions that have had to reform themselves, or perish. We will observe how the new technologies are creating new learning forms. Finally, we will explore what education might look like in the future using Internet portals.

We ask only that the reader open his or her mind to let these thoughts roll through. Check them against the reality of your own knowledge of schooling, and try out our suggested path for educational reform. By the time you finish reading *Leaving School: Finding Education,* we hope you will be ready to begin the search for a new way of learning in the 21st century.

Chapter One

Openers

> Defining change in terms of a school is both
> hopeless and self-defeating. The school can't be
> fixed, but education in America can be reformed.

The time has arrived for the United States to think seriously about bidding farewell to its schools. Our nation's largest and most time-honored institution, housing some fifty-seven million students each day, is a relic from another age. The school is responsible for increasing amounts of cultural decay and social dysfunction in our society. The curriculum found in today's school is programming our children for the past, not the present, and certainly not the future. Parents, knowledgeable educators, and savvy business leaders must begin a serious search for a different medium for educating our children.

A major paradigm shift, or change in perspective, has occurred in the last decade using the new technologies. This shift represents an opportunity to redesign the way in which we learn and transmit culture to our children. The school we all know, formed in the 19th century, survives as an institution in the 21st century from sheer habit. While business, the government, the military, transportation, telecommunications, and most other institutions in our nation are applying these new technologies to handle the complex operational changes in every day life, schools are not. Schools remain frozen in place without vision, a symbol of another age. The status of the school as America's last operating institutional monopoly suppresses any genuine motivation to modernize.

Technology, at the heart of the phenomenal transformation being experienced in America, is now found in every corner of American society. These new technologies are responsible for the fundamental changes occurring in the way we do things every day, pushing out our old ways of thinking and acting. For example, sending mail through the U.S. Postal System has given way to seventeen million email messages every day in the United States. The change is truly revolutionary.

Signs of this new technological age are visible throughout American society in the first years of this new millennium. Transportation has become highly computerized in its schedules and routes, on land and in the air. Agriculture is now a high-tech and worldwide corporate endeavor. Medicine routinely uses technologies in scanning, cloning, and transplanting parts of the human body. Our military uses laser beams, computers, and satellites to wage wars on a global scale with minimal loss of life. Even individual citizens proceed through the day armed with laptops, palm pilots, and cell phones. The school, however, is distinctive in the retention of its 19th century procedures and concerns. The new technologies have not significantly impacted its operations.

Despite the appearance of success in educating so many students each day, our schools are in serious decline and have been for almost half a century. The final shift in the control of schools during the 1980s, from local agencies to state bureaucracies, has resulted in schools becoming both fiscal and political prisoners of government. Special pleadings and whimsical legislation now act to enforce a kind of irrationality for all schools. The many battles for values in America – sex education, integration, exceptional education – are fought out in the courts and applied in the schools. There is a constant jerky and piecemeal change occurring in the individual schools that comprise this huge institution so in need of fixing. Our schools have no true hope of reforming themselves. There has not been a lasting change in half a century. Schools cannot and will not change!

The institutional perspective of schools and their leaders is myopic at best. The mind set is a year-to-year, season-to-season operation. The lengthy history of education in America and our previous experiences with change in schools, has delayed our even being able to see the new technologies as an option for future learning. Schools, as they address technology, are focused on the "yes, but" aspects of change. Curriculum filters are far more important than curriculum futures. Regulation and security are on the front burners. Schools are resistant to changing; they have always been this way. Educators fought against ballpoint pens and hand-held calculators as well. At best, technology in schools is about being faster at doing old things. Our paradigms have failed us.

The critical problem is that schools can't "see" the new technologies for what they have become. In society-at-large, technology is the medium that is changing how people live and work and what they do with their spare time. Schools are not preparing students with the skills and perceptions to survive in such a fast moving world. Parents should be both frightened and outraged at this lack of relevance and this leadership incompetence. Perhaps as a result of the world in which we are living, parents feel powerless to intercede.

Consider the fact, for example, that each day there are three million new web pages on the Internet. At the time of this writing, in fact, there are now more web pages on the Internet than there are persons on Earth. The English Internet, or World Wide Web, is doubling every 120 days, or three times each year. Some 80 percent of all the web pages that will be available to learners next year don't yet exist! Nearly one billion persons around the world are regular users of the Internet after only nine years of availability (May 1995). Most children, at least in school, are not part of this phenomenal transformation in communication. How can this be? The answer is simple: schools are so large, so much a monopoly in the learning game, that they don't even acknowledge Internet resources as a competitor. Schools are the largest impeding force in our nation as we move into the information age.

Both of the authors of this book have worked in schools as agents of change for over thirty years. We believe that education in the United States can reform and modernize itself, given the right opportunity. But our joint conclusion, after working so many years with schools throughout the United States and in many foreign lands, is that such reform will be successful only if we can shed the school as our learning vessel. In the case of schools, function is following form, and the "school" in its form is blocking our transition to electronic-assisted learning in the 21st century.

Even if there were no technological "issues" for educational reform, the authors believe that the United States may soon have to abandon its schools anyway. In a kind of "black hole" scenario, it is likely that schools would collapse under their own weight in the near future. Schools are becoming intolerably expensive and so issue-oriented that they are beginning to pull other institutional agencies downward in a fiscal spiral. In state after state, legislators are wrestling with the cost of schools in direct competition with health, law enforcement, and government benefits. There simply isn't enough pie to continue as we have in the past.

A quick profile of the state of American education using the federal government's National Center for Educational Statistics (2002) reveals that this institution is, indeed, a sick puppy. Education in America has always been expensive; approximately 80 percent of all expenditures are for salaries and facilities. Since 1970, the expenditures for schooling have grown in a geometric pattern as shown by these figures:

1970	$100 billion
1980	$200 billion
1990	$400 billion
2000	$750 billion

Anyone who believes that the United States will find an additional $750 billion to cover the growth of education (60 percent public elementary and secondary schools) by 2010 is sadly out-of-touch with the fiscal debates at various levels of government. The geometric progression is simply frightening.

Of course, the need for buildings and teachers is largely determined by the number of students being served by our educational systems. And, while private education enrollment in the United States has been arrested at 11 percent since 1985, the public system has been growing steadily. Today's tax-supported public schools are educating 47.7 million students in 91,380 school buildings. Factoring in inflation, the cost of serving all of these students is nearly double today what it was in 1985.

Our fifty state systems are spending more and more per pupil, with cost being calculated by either a per pupil cost or, more common, an average daily attendance cost (ADA). In 1986, the cost per pupil using ADA was $3756 per year. In 2003, the cost per pupil, in current dollars, is approaching $8400. The increase has been slow but steady as shown below:

1986	$3756
1988	$4240
1990	$4980

1992	$5421
1994	$5767
1996	$6147
1998	$6675
2000	$7237
2002	$8077

These projections, of course, continue upward with an estimated cost per pupil in 2005 of $9232. Every child in school after 2003, if they complete all twelve years of required attendance, will cost more than $100,000 to educate. Complicating taxpayer support for these increases is the fact that the majority of these children who have been added since 1986 are immigrants, children not born of American parents with full citizenship.

The ethnicity composition for public school children since 1972 shows a 17 percent increase in "minority children." As a total group, minority children now represent a whopping 39 percent of all public school students, with the largest concentrations in the South (49 percent) and the West (45 percent). Five states (Texas, California, New York, Hawaii, Louisiana), plus the District of Columbia, have no majority (at least 50 percent) students. In fifty of our largest cities, minority children represent the new "minority majority." For example:

Miami	87.8%
Washington, D.C.	84.7%
Detroit	80.1%
Atlanta	70.3%
Los Angeles	62.7%
Chicago	62.1%
Houston	59.6%
San Francisco	53.4%

These figures, however, provide only a partial picture of the problem. Because most of this rapid population growth has been comprised of young students (preschool and lower elementary grades), the new population "wave" will have to be accommodated at each successive level of education (elementary, middle, secondary) by building schools and hiring teachers. Building needs and teacher shortages are already a tremendous problem for schools in most states. The prospect of states being able to fund these needs in the immediate future (now) looks bleak.

Since the so-called "return to the basics" movement in the 1980s, schools have been badly underfunded for facility maintenance, repair, and replacement. At present, the National Education Association is warning of a nationwide school infrastructure crisis. In their 2001 study *Modernizing Our Schools: What Will It Cost?* the NEA estimated that to repair, renovate, and build needed schools, and to equip them with modern technology, would cost approximately $322 billion. This estimate is three times what previous government estimates have been, and roughly ten times as much as states are currently spending to fix or build schools.

A second economic force squeezing our public and private schools is the growing cost of the teaching force. In the short twelve-year period from 1990-2002, America's public schools have increased the number of teachers in the classroom by a whopping 29 percent. This growth matched the new enrollment growth caused by immigration, and came at a time when the average salary for teachers almost doubled. Today, using a ballpark figure of $50,000 per teaching unit (includes retirement and benefits), one can only gasp at the true cost of adding nearly one million teachers during this period.

An example of how much financial pressure is facing schools can be found in the simple increase in health care premiums for teachers in Dade County (Miami) schools, a district of three hundred thousand pupils. For the 2002-2003 school year alone, coverage for teachers required an additional

$28 million. Health costs, of course, compete directly with school costs in government budgets.

The difficulty of using such a "business model" to calculate costs in education is, of course, that schools are not businesses. You cannot simply calculate the number of pupils arriving, then the number of buildings and teachers needed, to gain some per unit cost. Kids are not widgets, and the reality is that school children do not all cost the same. Two specific examples can be cited to demonstrate this fact. First, in 1975, and again in 1990, the federal government (Congress) passed legislation to recognize and service children with learning disabilities. In 2003, these children numbered about 14 percent of the entire public school population (over 6.5 million), and their cost was weighted by their type of disability. If a child had a regular disability or was emotionally disturbed, the cost might be only twice as much as a non-categorical (normal) student. If, however, the child was severely handicapped (autistic), blind, or homebound, the cost could be up to ten times more than for a child without such a disability. Schools have wrestled, unsuccessfully, with the fiscal dimensions of these laws for a quarter of a century.

The second difficulty is that many of those newly arrived students in our public schools since 1986, are high maintenance students. Many are language "challenged." In America, about 15 percent of all children come from homes where the income falls below the poverty line, but where immigrants cluster (the cities) or growth is rapid (the jobs), this figure can average about 30 percent (Florida). For taxpayers in such areas (the Sun Belt), this reality results in many high cost students requiring special programs. And, all things being equal, the income level of the parent is the best single predictor of success or failure in school.

It can be said that the more poor children a school, district, or state has, the less successful it will be in educating those children. Our national drop out rate of 30 percent (Grades 9-12) is much higher in some parts of the country. In areas with high Hispanic populations, the drop out rate can approach 50 percent of all students. Throughout the United States, children in the lower 20 percent of family income are five times more likely to drop out of school than their counterparts in the upper 20 percent of family income.

From a business standpoint, spending $50,000 to $75,000 on a drop out is preposterous. A "no-brainer." There is no product. No accountability. There is only waste. Such a senseless extravagance simply cannot continue indefinitely.

And, to complete this picture of money wasted and lives ruined, it can be observed that in the period 1985-1997, only 4 percent of those persons under eighteen years old sent to prison were high school graduates. Of the two million persons incarcerated in the United States, the vast majority are high school drop outs; and this group is very disproportionately minority. When a student drops out of school and ends up in prison, the cost to the taxpayer is about five times greater upon arrival. Systematically, beginning with the schools, we indebt our nation through a chain of foul-ups.

Likewise, it is very difficult to employ a business model when speaking of the nearly three million classroom teachers we hire to teach our children. This labor force, the only all-college graduate labor force in America, has been a kind of "spit-n-cobwebs" network of good people holding together a creaking institution for nearly fifty years. At about $50,000 per unit, teachers have represented one of the grand bargains for the taxpayer for a very long time. But the good old days of "dedicated slaves" is nearly over, and the teachers are beginning to tilt badly toward getting out of schools.

Schools have always been staffed by upstanding and dedicated professionals who have endured low pay and terrible work conditions to assist youth. Ninety percent female, this highly reliable workforce, this social safety net, is breaking under the strain. In a 2002 study of teachers entitled *Why Are Experienced Teachers Leaving the Profession*, it was found that a real teacher shortage was upon us, aggravated by a veteran staff of millions who wished they were somewhere else.

The study found a similarity, of all things, in the attitudes of solid classroom teachers and the attitudes of school drop outs! Both groups reported feelings of alienation (isolation, normlessness, powerlessness, and irrelevance) that were shockingly widespread. The number one reason given by both teachers and students for dropping out or wanting out of school was the low-level mission of today's schools. The teachers identified minimum standards curriculum, excessive testing and bureaucratic demands (paperwork) as the chief irritants. These were followed closely in the survey by the bad attitudes of students, parents, and administrators regarding their efforts. Stated simply, teachers are getting no respect for their heroic efforts to teach a scholars' curriculum to America's coarse and dynamic populations. The observations of the teachers in this survey confirm what is widely known in the profession; the nature of the job has changed and the new world of teaching isn't pretty.

As one teacher in this survey observed, "When Laura Bush [President George W. Bush's wife] goes on TV to recruit the 'best and the brightest' to teaching for two years, the implication is that, after two years, these people have done their public service and now can go on to real jobs that pay a decent wage. The other implication is that the best and the brightest don't choose teaching – that's insulting."

A classroom teacher well known to the authors, likened the new elementary school classroom to an old I Love Lucy routine:

It is 8:20 in the morning and I am already exhausted and frustrated. My students know this; it is not their fault. We have turned our Schools into businesses and little factories.

I run in the back gate carrying a bag far too heavy for me. I left school at 6:15 yesterday afternoon with a three-hour stack of papers left to grade and notes still to be written to each parent. I also had some work to do on my computer for my micro-economy class (required).

I put assignments on the board, put them on the computer, put away graded papers, leave notes on a few desks, answer two phone calls, check my email and select the most important ones from the sixty that have accumulated since yesterday afternoon. I also check my voice mail and pray that none of them needs immediate attention. The replies to these will consume my twenty-five minute lunch break.

I grab papers to run off for next week, hang a banner on the door, and dash off to the office to check my mailbox and turn in the runoffs. I arrive late to pick up my thirty students from the holding area, answer numerous questions on the way to class, stop to respond to a logistical question from two teachers, and do my best to get into my room before student dismissal.

In the room I hurry past the children to turn on the TV (with the sound off so we can hear the intercom announcements). As my wonderful students line up to leave the home room, they ask me questions, query me about reminders on their desk, hand me homework, and let me know about their latest crises (home fights, upset tummies, disappearing homework). As I speak to as many students as possible, the intercom comes on. Helpers are passing out assignments, graded papers, and filling out planners. I ask them all to stop what they are doing and sit down.

We are reminded to take popcorn orders, send in the red and white count (percent of students wearing school colors), and details about the Olympic torch runner who will pass the school today. I am then reminded to turn up the volume on the TV for the morning news. I dash to the back of the room to man the television buttons.

As soon as the announcements cease, I begin madly collecting money for popcorn, getting the red and white count, filling out the attendance report, collecting notes on how many students are going home today or why they weren't at school yesterday, and determine which of the three entrees our students will want for lunch today – all while the school patrol and late arrivals drift into the room. The custodian is outside the open door, but I can't hear what he is telling me. I stop what I am doing to respond to his observation, and then shut the door so I can hear the children again.

The intercom is coming back on!

After the lunch count for the third time (students keep arriving), I ask again if I got all the popcorn orders? Other students help me collect forms for the weekly report, the field trip, and the parent luncheon next week. A futile attempt is made to check our academic planners.

The exceptional education teacher enters my room and asks to see one of my pupils. We conference on the spot about his missing work and decide that he should work on it now rather than going to chorus rehearsal.

A call from the office countermands our decision – the music teacher has requested that he be allowed to practice this morning. The exceptional teacher is told to email all missing work to the office and to accompany the student to the music room. She wants to know if I have his assignments to make up for this missed period. I reply that I'll have to get them to her later.

It is now 8:10 and two students have entered my room and are standing impatiently by the door; they obviously have a very important mission to accomplish. I ask them if I can help as someone hands me money for something – heaven help me if I leave a name off the lunch list. The messengers tell me that the music teacher really needs his students NOW. They were supposed to be in his room at 8:05!

At light speed I check with my chorus students about their completed work, remind them to line up in alphabetical order as required, and send them on their way. It is 8:15, and the intercom is barking orders about where the popcorn money should be taken, and informing me that a parent has left someone's lunch for them in the office.

My hair is turning red; I watch the unwrapped candies roll by faster than I can wrap them! They're falling off the conveyor belt; I start popping them into my mouth, hastily wrapping any I can grab. They're getting by, and I just can't seem to get my job done!

It is 8:20, and I'm tired. Thank goodness for the candy that does get wrapped. I really love to teach. If only I could wrap them all.

Certainly, we could go on. Old facilities, no technology, needy students, overworked teachers, irate parents, inconsiderate administrators, drop outs, lousy test scores, crime, pesky politicians, and expensive as hell. This is an institution, your authors believe, in its final days. An alternative must be found – quickly. We are running out of time and money, and the conditions we are describing are stressing both the American economy and its culture. School's inability to join the new technological age in America, its final hope for reform, is the proverbial "last straw."

While many educators in the past century have called for the reform of the school, your authors do not. What we believe, after very full careers in schools as teachers, administrators, and curriculum leaders, is that defining any improvement in the school will be both a futile exercise and a self-defeating proposition. The American school cannot be fixed, but American education can be reformed. We believe the United States must seriously explore abandoning the school as the vessel for learning and move to redefine education in terms of other options. We believe that a failure to break away, soon, will result in a surprisingly rapid deterioration of this institution, and the even further decline of the general culture of the United States.

Educators, parents, and business leaders in the United States must first recognize that we are being guided by old mental patterns, by false and obsolete paradigms. Just as the French army expected the Maginot Line of fortified trenches to stop the German Blitzkrieg at the beginning of World War Two, we still expect our schools to muddle through at the dawn of the information age. This hope that schools, as they exist, can adequately prepare our children for the future is false and unrealistic. American education, our schools, has been a non-performing institution in meeting this responsibility since 1980 when our leaders stuck their heads in the sands of standardized testing and minimal competence curriculums.

There are signs, hopeful indicators we think, that our nation may be ready for a real change in the way we educate our children. Those citizens with vision will find the ideas in subsequent chapters refreshing and insightful. Career school personnel, government agents, university scholars, publishers of textbooks, and other groups heavily vested in the old ways will probably not be able to even imagine that real change is possible. Blinded by their old paradigm that schools equal education, these groups will opt to hang onto older and obsolete learning procedures.

A great deal is at stake in the coming discussions about leaving our schools behind. The authors hope that parents, wishing the best for their children, will ultimately demand a modern and relevant system of education. These parents can, and must, become strong consumer advocates and critics of the unbearable status quo. With the assistance of knowledgeable educators and informed business leaders, America can shed its final monopoly, its antique school system, and reform education for the 21st century.

Telesurgery Revolutionizes Medicine

On September 7, 2001, a 68-year-old woman in Strasburg, France, had her gall bladder removed. The surgeons performing the operation were nearly 4,000 miles away in New York. Jacques Marescaux from the European Institute of Telesurgery teamed up with New York surgeon Michael Gagner, to perform the first complete telesurgery procedure performed by surgeons miles from the location of their patient. Gagner and Marescaux performed the historic long-distance operation using a high-speed fiber optic service deployed by France Telecom. The two surgeons controlled the instruments using an advanced robotic surgical system, designed by Computer Motion, Inc., that enabled the procedure to be minimally invasive. The patient was released from the hospital after 48 hours and was able to resume normal activity the following week.

The historic operation was made possible by a new high-speed fiber-optic connection between France and New York. The key obstacle to telesurgery had been time delay. It is critical that a continuous time delay of less than 200 milliseconds be maintained throughout the procedure between the surgeon's movements and the video images on his screen in New York. Said Marescaux. "I felt as comfortable operating on my patient as if I had been in the same room."

Highly skilled surgeons will soon be able to perform difficult operations through these long-distance procedures. The computer systems used to control surgical instruments can also be a part of breakthrough techniques for teaching a whole generation of medical practitioners.

Source: France Telecom North America, IRCAD European Institute for Telesurgery.

Chapter Two

Second to None

> If our nation had stopped developing around 1900, the United States would possess the finest education system in the world.

America has always possessed a rather amazing education system. Just sixteen years after the Pilgrims landed at Plymouth Rock (1620), America had both primary schools and the first institution of higher education. By the beginning of the 20th century, free and universal public education was a fact of life in the United States. One hundred years later, at the dawn of the 21st century, our system of education is the envy of the modern world. Each day, fifty-seven million people go to school for an education in the United States. The destiny of our nation and its system of schools have always been wedded together in a symbiotic relationship; schools have been, from the very beginning, the strength and the miracle of America.

Having made these lofty observations, your authors must also state that they believe the schools of America are now in a dysfunctional state. These miracles of the 19th and the 20th centuries may soon do us in. That period in the 19th century when the present school form was "locked in" has vanished. Change in our society, real and perceived, has caused most institutions in our country to radically alter the way they operate. Various "paradigm" shifts, defined as changed in perceptions or assumptions about our world, have altered the operation and the purpose of most businesses and social services. Schools in America, and most other nations, have not responded or adapted to these shifts.

To fully understand how our schools can be second to none and, at the same time, dangerous to our nation's survival, we must focus on how our schools were developed, and how they are presently perceived by citizens of the United States. What underlying assumptions do Americans have about their schools, and how accurate are these perceptions that guide our behaviors toward this bedrock institution?

We can discuss schools in the United States in terms of three distinct stages of development, the third of which is presently unfolding as we experience the first decade of this new century. The first stage began in the early colonies and consisted of establishing a "system" of education (Grades 1-12) that was largely completed at the end of the 19th century. The second stage, which occupied most of the 20th century, refined and honed that early education system in ways that will prove familiar to most living adults. The final stage, just beginning, will work toward disassembling the original 19th century model and replacing it with some kind of new system reflective of the massive changes occurring in our world at this time. Schools, as we know them, must soon change or disappear.

The Period of Building

Most educators can tell you that, in the beginning (1635), the early colonist built schools similar to what they had known in Europe. These so-called Latin Grammar Schools were "reading" and "writing" schools; the popular motivation for establishing such schools was to promote religion. Following Martin Luther's prescription, readers who could access God's word in the Bible could "ward off" the evils of the Devil himself. Under early legislation, such as the Old Deluder Satan Act (1647), schools were erected.

By 1650, the Massachusetts Bay Colony had mandated that, any place where fifty families were located, a school would be established and a tax levied to support the school. The other colonies quickly followed this lead. Incredibly, this was one hundred and forty years before the United States Constitution was ratified – and these were the very people who had come to the new world to escape taxation and religious tyranny.

Paralleling the establishment of the popular schools, which would grow into a complete 1-12 graded system by the end of the 19th century, was the private system of higher education. The establishment of Harvard University (1636) was soon followed by other "ivy league" universities and later by public colleges and universities. The origin of these schools was not connected in any way to the establishment of the lower schools. These first universities were modeled on emerging universities in Europe where the leaders of religion and state were trained.

We mention the odd fact that two separate and different education systems took root in America simultaneously because they would grow into two distinct and fairly incompatible philosophies for education by the 20th century. The public schools were of the Roman model (educating the masses of the empire), as contrasted with the colleges and universities, which modeled themselves on the elite system of Greece where only the few were highly educated.

America would support both of these approaches to education in their development; combined they would eventually become one massive kindergarten through college system. But these two systems, when merged the "American way," would only co-exist, and this incompatibility is one of the root causes of the dysfunction in today's schools.

The growth of the American system was uneven and seemed to lurch along in fifty-year increments. By 1750 (forty years before the United States was founded), the public system was established through the elementary grades, and tutors and private academies were serving as bridges upward to the university levels. By 1821, the first public-supported high school was in place, and by 1850, compulsory education laws were being passed throughout the country. The Kalamazoo Case (Michigan State Supreme Court, 1874) determined the right of states to tax for the support of secondary education – the rest, as they say, is history. By 1890, most states had an elementary and a secondary education system supported by taxation, as well as both a public and private system of higher education.

The termination of this first stage of education development in America occurred in 1892, when the presidents of Harvard and other private colleges (The Committee of Ten) met to establish college entrance requirements. The committee mandated specific courses and, when defined by time requirements (the Carnegie units), such courses became the high school curriculum so familiar to all of us today. High schools throughout the nation adopted these university-mandated requirements so that their students could gain access to the upper level "elite" system of private and public colleges.

In just a little over two hundred years, the United States possessed a powerful nation-building vehicle. This comprehensive system was both public and private, separate from control by any church, decentralized to the state level (education was not mentioned in the Constitution, thus was a state's right), supported by taxation, and mandatory for all. The American education system turned out large numbers of highly educated graduates who could fill the leadership roles of an expanding nation while, at the same time, providing a general education for all of those citizens living in an experimental democracy. The system was unique and seemingly perfect.

If our nation had stopped developing in 1900, the United States would have possessed the finest education system in the world. And, in fact, as we enter the 21st century, it is probable that America has the best overall education in the world by any definition. We educate more people, longer, than any other country on earth. Our facilities, teacher-training colleges, and universities are the envy of most nations. Students from foreign lands still struggle to get into the United States to attend this system of education. So, what's the problem?

Unfortunately, our nation did not arrest its development in 1900, and the entire 20th century could be characterized as a second period in which educators tried to "fit" their education system to a rapidly changing world. In hindsight, such adaptation was a nearly impossible task.

The Period of Refinement

Looking back a century, only a short while but it seems like forever, we can see the old system of educating tooled up and operating smoothly. At the end of the 19th century, most Americans (90 percent who lived on farms) went to school for eight years, and a few (two hundred thousand) went on to high school. Far fewer, of course, attended or completed college. Given this large lower education system and the tiny upper education system, there was little or no conflict between the vastly different forms and purposes of each level.

Once secondary education was supported by public taxation, however, the high school enrollments soared (five million by 1920), and the elite system of studies began to prove inappropriate for the general population. The growth era, beginning one hundred years ago, had the misfortune to "bloom" just as the United States was transitioning from an agricultural society to an industrial society. Change, in the form of heavy immigration, population mobility from the farms to the cities, an increase in the use of machines in production, and new and radical ideas about education coming from Europe, was everywhere. In twenty short years, one generation (1900-1920), the educational system of the United States became unstable as traditional values about "schooling" changed.

In 1900, an industrial revolution was fully underway in the United States and work was becoming mechanized. While there were miracle machines in this period, such as the automobile and the airplane, less spectacular machines transformed the workplace. Human labor, when needed, became specialized, and the backbreaking labor was largely eradicated. Assembly lines and autocratic structures for efficiency appeared in American factories, and the country began to become wealthy beyond its wildest dreams.

Today's public schools, the ones we all know, were formed during this period. Taking their cues from factory efficiency and organization, and following the dictates of Scientific Management principles, schools were organized as little businesses. Students were seen as "products" moving through the grades, being assessed and certified. This "knowledge factory" employed structure in its facilities, teaching methodologies, and evaluation criteria to be successful. The education business grew by expansion – not adaptation to the environment. More was better. Longevity was stability.

There was the beginning of a curriculum transformation during this period. Subjects such as English, social studies, art, music, physical education, and vocational studies were added from necessity. For example, one-half of all recruits failed the physical exam in World War One, which led to the introduction of physical education in schools. But this growth in the curriculum, and the expansion of teaching methodologies, was reactive and piecemeal, a sort of accretion process where new things were added to old things without serious concern for the outcomes.

The so-called "progressive" educational ideas from Europe did make some inroads at the elementary level during this period, which meant some new school forms and methods of teaching. Some innovation was evident at the secondary level as well, but always as an add-on to the traditional structures of the 1890s. By the end of the 1920s, the American school was becoming a true hybrid: a traditional education stalk with a graft of child-centeredness attached. While always an appendage to the traditional system of educating, this new and responsive wing of American education was, by 1920, a permanent fixture in our schools.

From 1920 to the 1950s, these two parallel and incompatible faces of American education co-existed uneasily. Two world wars, a depression, and a dynamic social milieu acted to hide these differences. One system, the traditional, focused on knowledge, and the other system, progressive, focused on student development. As the following chapter will show, such incompatibility could only be masked by expenditures of funds sufficient to support these parallel systems simultaneously. In the best of times, the progressive elements of the new system would emerge and flourish. When the economy was not so good, child-centered programs would struggle and recede into the shadows.

By the middle of the 20th century, it was clear that the traditional and progressive wings of American education served very different masters. As early as the 1950s, it was evident that schooling was becoming horribly expensive and that funds for education were not unlimited. Still, the dilemma of rising costs and unclear purpose in schools was often masked by events in society at large, such as the entry of the federal government into educational funding, the influence of the courts in defining education, and direct competition of other social agencies (such as health and the military) for the same funds.

Starting in this time period, and continuing for fifty years, American education began an era of decline. The progressive and humanistic education model stalled, and traditional education questioned itself publicly. By 1980, neither of the two wings of American education was experiencing health; this stagnation reflected greater America, no longer dynamic, slowing to a near crawl.

The Period of Decline and Disassembly

The period of 1980-2000, recent history, witnessed the wholesale retreat of progressive education and the almost total withdrawal of the school system from any kind of environmental adaptation to the change about it. Schools, from 1980 onward, did not accommodate the many staggering paradigm shifts experienced by our nation and did not participate in the emerging techno-revolution as our society entered the information age. Rather, schools became more bureaucratic and narrow in addressing the business of teaching and learning. School leaders, under great pressure from government and business, fell back on managerial structures of the early 20th century (a return to roots). The great American education system, second to none, was dying!

Caught in the crossfire of increasing costs and decreasing achievement, schools in the 1980s retreated to the same business model they had emulated at the beginning of the 20th century. The new code words were "accountability" and "back to the basics," but in reality, our educational leaders were badly lost and divided. Lacking a clear philosophy, and possessing only a murky understanding of the true power of the teaching/learning act, educational leaders abdicated their responsibilities to state legislatures who were now the chief financiers of public schooling. These elected officials, spouting business slogans, called for increased testing and standardization of the curriculum in the pursuit of "higher scores." The winding down of the existing schooling models was surprisingly quick under the conservative influences of the "right-wing" politicians. The "system" began to refine itself into a state of obsolescence.

As the new schooling programs focused on test scores and narrow outcomes, most of the changes that might have influenced education were ignored. This was particularly true of the granddaddy of all paradigm shifts in America, the entry of the new technologies. In a rarely understood development, computers became personal learning tools with the advent of the Internet.

In schools, educators saw the early computers as simply another way in which standardized learning could be promoted. Schools rushed to set up computer "labs" where children could be assembled to "drill" on the basics. Having programmed the schools to use computers to promote standardized basic skill mastery, educators were unable to "let go" and reprogram their budgets for a new purpose. With the Internet (1995), the computer was a personal learning machine capable of reaching a long-standing dream of assisting each child in his or her own growth. Unfortunately for us all, the traditionalists were fully in charge of schools during this period, and their knowledge-biased perceptions of schooling prevented them from recognizing this change. By the year 2000, it was obvious that schools had missed this opportunity completely, relegating them to obsolescence in a rapidly changing world.

How Did It Happen?

The decline of the American public school system actually began at the end of the 19th century when reforms fell woefully short of what was needed. A complete redesign of education was called for as our society transitioned from agricultural to industrial – but such change was not forthcoming. In fact, the decline went completely unnoticed due to the business model lens through which schools were viewed. Enrollments skyrocketed, school buildings were constructed, millions of teachers were trained, and public tax contributions to education rose steadily for nearly fifty years. From the business model perspective things looked great.

Unfortunately, in the middle of all of that growth of the first fifty years of the 20th century, our nation changed, and the role of schools was altered. The true client of schooling, the child, was discovered, but never serviced. Schools continued to organize learning for the purpose of producing workers and little scholars. Schools were about sorting and selecting, winning and losing. In short, somewhere early in the 20th century, the elite system of the early universities overrode the popular system of the early public schools. It would take nearly a century for this fatal flaw to reveal itself fully.

To understand what was at stake during the early days of decline, 1900-1950, we must look beyond the business model and employ a different paradigm. Certainly, from the business model, many schools were built and more students came and stayed longer in schools. And, yes, the high literacy rate in America by mid-century was the envy of the world. However, the price of this efficiency, this standardization in learning, was a loss of effectiveness. Schools became better and better at turning out academic units – graduates who knew the strange things identified by the Committee of Ten but couldn't actually do anything! Schooling failed miserably in meeting the needs of its clients and in serving its sponsors, the taxpayers of the United States.

From the time of the Greeks, there have been differences of opinion about man and his education. These differences can be seen clearly in contrasting Aristotle's *Politics* with Plato's *Republic*. Aristotle believed that man was born bad, or fundamentally flawed, and was redeemed by society. Plato, by contrast, believed that man was born good and was corrupted by society. Aristoteleans are natural conservatives, while Platonians are natural reformers. These two opposing views of man suggest two very different ways of educating children: shaping them or setting them free. In Europe in the 19th century, these ideas of man's goodness (Platonian) and the notion of a facilitating school found form in writing, and soon were adopted by some American educators.

These European writings, including Pestalozzi, Froebels, and Rousseau, came to America as an educational exhibit at our Centennial Celebration (1876) in Philadelphia. The ideas floated for about twenty years before being re-written and promoted by John Dewey, a legendary educator. Dewey directed attention away from content as the focus of schooling by demonstrating a new and different kind of "child-centered" curriculum at the Lab School of the University of Chicago (1896-1904).

Before Dewey, as recently as a century ago, children were perceived as incomplete people (little adults) who possessed an evil spirit (beat the devil out of them) and who needed to be both filled up and corrected. The school, as an agent of adults, was to accomplish this filling and correcting with as much efficiency as possible. The Europeans, however, referred to the child as good, not bad, and recognized the uniqueness of childhood. They called for a "growing" curriculum, one that would allow each child to unfold in his or her own way. To state the obvious, these were incompatible conceptions of reality.

Dewey transformed the ideas of the Europeans into a general conception of school as a place where students were served. As a philosopher, psychologist, and educator rolled into one, Dewey called for a curriculum in which real life (not dry subjects) was present, and where the child, not the teacher, was the center of the teaching-learning process.

In his best-known book, *Democracy and Education* (1916), Dewey connected the schooling process with the unique form of government found in the United States. In our democratic form of government, he observed, it is necessary for citizens to participate and to understand the changes occurring about them. Our citizens, he stated, live in a dynamic and changing environment, and must be taught to adapt and to think for themselves. In making this connection, Dewey tied school to the future, not the past, and advocated an active and practical wisdom to be taught in schools.

These ideas, over a two-decade period, challenged the traditional educators and their ways of teaching and learning. Subjects were added to the curriculum, and more modern methods of teaching replaced the Socratic lecture format that had characterized teaching in the 19th century. By the mid-1920s, American schools were both traditional and dynamic, a combination that paid dividends for the nation as a world leader. Our graduates were inventive, spontaneous, adventuresome and flexible. They acted in ways so – well – "American."

This blend of educational approaches provided a near perfect link to the capitalist economic system evolving during this same period. This concept of school successfully connected the seemingly disastrous paradox of the United States: social equality alongside economic competition.

Along the road to this new and exciting American model of educating, however, were three terrible events: World War One, the Great Depression, and World War Two. These national concerns eroded otherwise successful reform in schools and forced government intervention in school operations. The relationship between the government and schools in America was largely undefined due to the "residual powers" clause of the Constitution, and state government funding in support of local schools was very weak. Early attempts by the federal government to intervene in school affairs were large ineffective. Assorted commissions appointed by government leaders would utter goals at regular intervals, without meaningful response from the schools.

A document that might have guided the true reform of schools in America at the onset of the 20th century was the *Seven Cardinal Principles of Secondary Education.* Unlike the work of the Committee of Ten in the 1890s, this document was produced by regular educators who formed the Committee to Reorganize Secondary Education. Meeting from 1913-1918, this committee envisioned a program of general education (Roman model) that would include areas such as health, basic skills, home membership, vocation, civic education, use of leisure, and ethical character. This prescription was the antithesis of the tight academic vision of the college presidents.

Unfortunately, the report of the *Seven Cardinal Principles* arrived just as the United States was joining World War One, and any momentum for reform that existed at this time was lost in the turmoil of the following years. Still, many of the ideas from these practitioners made their way into the curriculum (adding physical education, vocational education, social studies) and were layered or superimposed on the old system of tight academic subjects.

Another good example of how the social dynamic, the environment, interfered with natural education evolution was the now classic research project known as both the Eight Year Study and the Thirty Schools Study. The study evolved from the Progressive movement of the 1920s, a period of considerable experimentation in our schools. The Progressives requested a period of freedom from the college entrance requirements (Committee of Ten) so that the truly innovative secondary schools could be studied for their effect on the performance of students in college. The traditionalists accepted the challenge.

The study matched some fifteen hundred pairs of students who went to either a traditional high school or an innovative secondary school, and then proceeded to college under this special admissions policy. The results of this eight-year study were remarkable. In every single category of comparison, except foreign language, the students who attended non-conventional secondary schools outperformed their statistical counterpart from a traditional high school when they attended college. This study alone should have caused a major redesign of the American high school. But it was the misfortune of this important study to conclude its findings in 1940, a time when war rather than education was on the minds of Americans. In addition, as always, there was no authoritative body to receive the findings. Though replicated later with the same general results, the Eight Year Study had no significant impact on American education.

A final example of how the reform of American education has been thwarted by the general social milieu, is found in the academic reforms of the late 1950s and early 1960s. Returning from World War Two, America found its education system strung out and badly watered down by attempts to combine the traditional education model with the progressive education model. The old curriculum still existed, but it was surrounded by an ever-growing co-curriculum comprised of add-on courses and social programs.

Serious efforts to return schools to a purely academic model were made by the then President of Harvard, James Conant, and the University of Chicago scholar, Mortimer Adler. The launch of Sputnik by the Russians in 1957 punctuated the need to "get going" again in the areas of math and science. New commissions and work groups met to create new curriculum materials later known as the "alphabet projects" (AAAS Science, PSSC Physicals, BSCS Biology, et cetera). These comprehensive redesigns of the school curriculum had the misfortune to arrive on the scene at the same time that the Brown versus Topeka Supreme Court ruling was beginning to be implemented. The efforts of the United States government to racially integrate all public schools in the late 1950s and 1960s simply took the steam out of academic reforms. Two very different agendas for schools proposed very different ways of educating our children; it was the elite Greek model versus the popular Roman model all over again.

In some ways, a rather glorious era of public school education transpired during these very confusing times. During the Kennedy and Johnson presidencies, massive sums of monies were supplied under the 1965 Elementary and Secondary Education Act to promote equality in educational opportunity. In order to meet the newly discovered cultural diversity, a concept of "public schools of choice" was promoted, setting a tone for over a decade of exploration and experimentation in curriculum development. Recognizing the early shift from the "melting pot" to the "salad bowl," Mario Fantini of the University of Massachusetts proposed that educators should create any curriculum desired by parents for their children. While such a concept sounds absurd today, it met the immediate needs of a nation rocking along with race riots and political discord. The "school of choice" concept would be reinvented in the 1980s and again in the 1990s as "magnet schools," "charter schools," and "voucher options."

The diversity of schools in America in the early 1970s, a time in which your authors were establishing their careers, was staggering. Under the loose phrase "alternative education," both public and private schools experimented with methods and designs. Some models were structured like the Berighter-Engleman special education program, which employed "head slaps" to correct misbehavior. Others are nearly existential free schools, such as those based on the Summerhill premises of individual freedom. In short, anything in the 1970s was permissible; the idea of an academic core for all American children all but disappeared.

To make things even more chaotic in the 1970s, the federal government was entering education as a reluctant funding partner to the states. Although this federal contribution to school funding never averaged more than 10 percent (more in poor districts), it was the court system that made Washington a significant player. Under the Great Society programs, federal access to schools, financial and otherwise, was mandated by repeated Supreme Court decisions. A notably liberal court during this period used the First and Fourteenth Amendments to guarantee student rights in schools. The financial contribution of the federal government was both the incentive and the means to enforce court mandates.

The federal government also applied funds to a number of areas of American schools to promote leadership, training, and research. For the first time, a cadre of "professional educators" were studying and changing schools. It is noteworthy that as this book is being written, most of those highly trained educators are retiring from the fray after working for more than thirty years, unsuccessfully, to alter the system and make it more progressive.

The United States' ability to financially carry two incompatible education systems simultaneously, as it had for decades, was rudely interrupted by the aftermath of the Vietnam War. The reader will remember that this war, which spanned the Kennedy, Johnson, and Nixon terms (1965-1972), was, above all else, costly. In the spirit of spend, spend, spend, these three administrations ran up a national debt in ways never seen before. It was a logical extension of this mind set that allowed public education to grow and expand unchecked for a full decade. When the true price tag for Vietnam became evident, in the form of both national debt and inflation, there was a rapid move to pull back and downsize in all walks of life, including education.

During the 1970s alone, there were eight straight years of 12 percent inflation. This meant that the dollar at the end of this period was worth only about one-half of its value at the beginning of the period. Schools, operating largely on property taxes and therefore always one year in arrears, faced massive shortfalls. The convergence of this fiscal calamity with a natural decline in the high school population and continually declining test scores on normed assessments (Scholastic Aptitude Test) made any further rationale for innovation impossible. Skyrocketing fiscal needs, fewer clients, and declining achievement sounded the end of independence for education in the United States. An era of accountability was long overdue, and it began with arguments over what constituted "basic."

If you were to ask any professional educator what was basic to education, you would receive a puzzled look. Of course, the first thing they would identify would be literacy skills (reading and writing), but beyond those two primary school subjects there would be a long list of contenders: vocational education, citizenship, home membership, personal development, lifetime learning skills, and others would compete for a place in the school curriculum. Ask anyone in the business community, by contrast, and you would get a very short list: basic work skills and more work skills.

Schools in the 1980s were tied by critics to the then bloated economy and faltering American productivity. This was the time of the Japanese car when Toyota, Honda, and Datsun captured one-half of the U.S. automobile market almost overnight. Our production capacities (steel for example) were declining or being moved overseas where cheap labor was present without troublesome unions. Failing businesses sought to downsize and refocus their missions. A highly conservative president was elected (Reagan), replacing another president who could not control inflation and the continuous growth of government.

Schools were particularly easy targets for downsizing because, during the 1970s, the primary responsibility for paying for schools had shifted from the local to the state level. Our state legislatures had only to use the money weapon to rein in school growth and experimentation. Legislators with no understanding of educational changes in 20th century railed against waste and called for holding schools accountable for their expenditures. The schools, they said, should abandon all of the "frills" and focus only on the basics. Like businesses, schools should have to justify expenditures with good old-fashioned results. Every school should be measured, counted, and held accountable.

Overnight, the businessman-legislator found educators who represented the most conservative fringe philosophies of education to propose new curricula. Best known among these statements was Mortimer Adler's (Professor at University of Chicago) *Paideia Proposal*. This "manifesto" called for a return to the 1890s curriculum or the Committee of Ten and suggested a curriculum focused solely on knowledge acquisition. The astounding thing about this widely discussed plan was that all children would have to master the same curriculum at the same level of achievement, "so that no child would be discriminated against." Eighty years of study concerning child development and differences in learning capacities was dismissed on the spot. We were back to filling up empty vessels.

Another tactic used to redirect the education establishment was to begin a pilot National Assessment Testing program (again, the University of Chicago) in basic subjects. This baseline of data was quickly connected to other achievement tests in mathematics and science so that American children could be compared to other students throughout the world. The phrase "world class education" began to buzz around. The working hypothesis of American business was, and still is, that American business could not be competitive in the world economy because our schools were failing. The many unfavorable comparisons of American students and students from other nations, given wide coverage in the conservative press, completely discredited American schools throughout the 1990s.

Perhaps the high water mark for this conservative campaign to capture our schools under the Regan administration was a report by the Commission on Excellence in Education. Entitled *A Nation At Risk*, this document began with the observation that if the enemies of the United States wished to destroy this country, they would create today's public schools. This opening paragraph was the "lead" story on education in the media for months.

Finally, in 1992, the U.S. Department of Labor issued its own recommendations for education in America under the label SCANS. This prescription called for a curriculum to create workers for industry, but failed to connect the prescription to the dawn of the information age in any significant way. What labor wanted was people who came to work, followed orders, and didn't get into trouble. This prescription was very much like the same Prussian method of organizing workers that gave form to our education system in the 19th century. In a frightening turn of events, the SCANS skills became the basis for school standards in many of our states.

Most professional educators, dedicated to years of study in human development and curricula innovation, viewed these reports as temporary reflections of the larger political scene. Looking back over the 20th century, there had been other times when the business elements had interceded to control schools and treat them like little businesses (1920s, 1950s). In fact, a kind of "wave theory" was held by most of those in the school world, as they were used seeing educational programming swing back and forth with the contracting or expanding economy. Surely, these ranting politicians and extreme right-wing educators would go away.

In retrospect, it is difficult to comprehend how successful the conservatives were in promoting their agenda from 1980-2000. In addition to buying or capturing the media, the schools, organized religion, and business, they also took control of the presidency, the U.S. Congress, the majority of governorships and state legislatures, and packed the Supreme Court of the United States. They did it with large sums of money, organization, and determination. In the education community they found no significant resistance. It was, as the saying goes, a "slam dunk."

Ultimately, from the ashes of the "basics" and "accountability" proposals came lasting change in the form of "standards." Using the same strategy practiced by the Committee of Ten one hundred years before, the legislatures of the United States began to set goals for the attainment of promotion, graduation, teacher pay, and a host of other measurable marks. Even when the attempts to establish a national set of goals failed (*National Education Goals – Goals 2000*, 1990), the various state legislatures coordinated their efforts through the chief school officers (various state commissioners of education) to establish state-level standards. Between laws and control of the budget, the two surest agents of change in education, schools were "squeezed down" and serious retrenchment was enacted.

It should be noted that the new standardized testing programs, which effectively narrowed the curriculum to rote teaching and learning, were not always above board. In many states, such testing opened a huge door for business to rush in and make a killing. In other states, such as Florida, the tests were used to discredit the public schools and open avenues for other conservative agendas such as school vouchers, the first step to privatization of the schools of the United States.

It was this constriction of the curriculum, using narrow standards to measure learning, which caused the United States educational establishment to miss the biggest paradigm shift in the history of learning. During that same 1980-2000 period when the conservatives were wrapping up the schools, the United States experienced the transition from a late industrial age society to a new information age society. The widespread use of the computer, followed by the onset of the Internet, totally altered how government, banks, the military, communications, and most other institutions operated. School leaders, preoccupied with complying with edicts from state legislatures, missed this transition completely. Schools today stand alone as the only major public institution in America not participating in the communication revolution. Overnight, schools transitioned from a cherished institution to our most dysfunctional public organization.

When computers first entered schools in the mid-1980s, they were perceived as administrative/business tools. School districts saw them as helpful in making payrolls, schedules, and keeping employee records. They were not immediately seen as something that might have value in classroom instruction. Later, in the 1980s, when personal computers (PCs) became available in stores, they were perceived in schools as a sort of status symbol. Individuals had these things, and the "best" schools had some. When they were obtained, schools would place them in prominent places, like the school office or library, to impress visitors. They were, of course, off-limits to students.

Eventually, the schools recognized that personal computers had some possibilities for the classroom. Apple Computer was the first company to provide meaningful instructional software for school use, and to this day is the preferred computer among teachers who use computers (less than half of all teachers) in an IBM world. But, because of the timing of their arrival, schools first saw computers as possible aids in teaching basic skills. After all, difficult and slow students seemed to respond to these machines better than they did to the dedicated teacher. Accordingly, most school districts proceeded to cluster these "teaching machines" in labs and treat the labs as basic skills labs (known as drill and kill in the business). A teacher (or aide even) assigned to the lab would oversee thirty or more students working their way through a fixed software package.

The development of the "lab approach," and the corresponding cottage industry of educational software companies that sprang up to service schools, continued to flourish from the mid-1980s to the mid-1990s. By this time, the investment in such machines was unbalancing school budgets and straining the capacity of schools to stay current in an industry (computers) with an eighteen-month horizon. Schools were racing down a dead-end street without a roadmap.

The Internet hit the United States with astounding speed in May of 1995. Within weeks of its arrival, all thinking about computers in America was altered. Although the Internet had been around since the Vietnam War (ARPANET), it had been exclusively a government and military tool until the late 1980s. At that point, scientists and some businesses were allowed to join in the flow of information (NSFNET). Finally, the Internet was released for public use by the U.S. Congress in the mid-1990s.

By this time, May 1995, standardized testing in schools was becoming an art form. Schools were "teaching to the test," whether standardized and normed like the SAT, or a homemade criterion-referenced and un-normed like most state achievement tests. The computer labs were a major part of this "war on ignorance," and schools found the computer-delivered basic skill instruction superior for most students. The arrival of the Internet, however, went largely unnoticed.

The geometric progress of persons in the United States using the Internet, as well as the astronomical number of websites available to users, meant that, by the late 1990s, the world of learning was taking off without schools. Students coming to school from homes with Internet connections were grossly advantaged in writing papers or researching subjects. Any student, with a few hours notice, could become nearly as knowledgeable (and sometimes more) as their teacher in niche information. Teachers naturally noticed this phenomena in a hurry, but were unable to much more than join the ranks of computer users with Internet connection by buying their own "at home" unit.

Throughout the 1990s and into today, public schools continued to buy expensive hardware for use in a lab setting, pulling wire through old buildings to get "hooked up." But in the new world, where schools are doing more and more to accomplish less and less, the Internet is something of a puzzle. The Internet, theoretically, could provide each student in America with a completely individualized education experience, as surely as each telephone exchange in the world has its own unique set of numbers. But, what good is the Internet to an educational system based on the 1890 industrial design of trying to standardize learning for all students? Our schools are, quite frankly, an anomaly.

Even worse, because of the legal nature of the schooling enterprise, and the self-imposed pressure to keep out of the public eye, most school leaders fear the Internet. There is, of course, the very real fact that perhaps one-third of all websites are pornographic or have "pop-ups" leading to a shadowy adult world. These can be controlled, for the most part, by various kinds of filters. But even more frightening, and dangerous to this nation, is the basic fear of educators that students might be able to learn without schools. This, your authors believe, is the real reason why our nation's schools have not entered the magic technological era like all the other institutions in our society. If students were able to access information from Internet-connected computers in school settings, the role of the teacher (knowledge dispenser) and the concept of a curriculum (pre-selected and fixed knowledge) would be undermined. Control would be lost; the school power badly diminished.

So, midway into the first decade of the 21st century, our schools have become technological dinosaurs. Computers in the school world are still drill masters, where ultra-violet zombies (students) sit in front of screens as workers sat before conveyor belts one century ago. Internet connections are locked down, screened out, filtered, even turned off. While a police car can pull up behind your vehicle at a red light and know in seconds if your vehicle is stolen, students are not allowed to communicate with others in this information-rich world. Learning occurs in schools, in buildings with seats in rows. Learning is what they tell you to know!

Early in this chapter it was observed that if the world arrested its development in 1905, school, as we now know it in the United States, would be the perfect institution. However, in a single century, the radio, television, airplane, satellites, computers, and a host of other new technologies have altered communication and the meaning of knowledge. On the learning horizon, about five years at best, we see more of this transition occurring. Presently, the largest single influence we see is the end of English language domination. Prior to 2004, the Internet was pretty much a western world phenomena, but after that date most users will not speak English as a first language. By 2020, most users on the Internet will be Chinese-speaking persons. The Internet will not go away; there will be multiple Internets, chock full of all of the knowledge the world possesses.

Students in school today will leave childhood to become adults in a world where acquisition of knowledge will take a back seat to utilization of knowledge. In such a world, schooling cannot be locked inside a physical factory-like structure that pretends to know all and be all. Each day of this century, the school that we know, America's pride and joy, slips further into oblivion. The school, our learning place, has become seriously dangerous to the programming of our nation's future.

The truly frightening thing about the disassembly of this largest of all national institutions, is that it is the economic rock of our nation. It is almost inconceivable that fifty-seven million students, nearly three million teachers, almost a hundred thousand school buildings, fleets of buses, thousands of teacher-training institutions, large publishing companies, and major segments of all state governments might not be engaged in running our schools. None of these groups can be counted on to "bite the hand that feeds them." All of these groups have a vested interest in seeing the school survive – no matter how dysfunctional it becomes!

In fact, only three kinds of people would support the removal of schools or a transition to a new kind of learning institution: entrepreneurial businessmen, irate taxpayers, and the parents of school children who want only the best for their child. The only other allies in the coming battle for the control of education in this nation are the professional educators themselves. No one, no other group, realizes how dysfunctional schools have become. There is a large and untapped reservoir of resistance to the schooling process inside our schools; like a genie in the bottle, many true educators detest what schools have become.

The authors do not believe that reform of schools from the inside is possible. During their careers, spanning thirty years, they have seen reform after reform fail. The authors do believe, however, that reform of education is possible. It can be accomplished quickly from the outside. It is time to bypass the school and find new educational avenues for our children. Our nation's future may depend on this alternative path being activated.

In the Virtual Courtroom

On April 1, 2001, a fictitious case was tried at the William and Mary Law School's McGlothin Courtroom in Williamsburg, Virginia. The defendants, witnesses, and attorneys were linked electronically to courtrooms in Leeds, United Kingdom, and Canberra, Australia. The proceedings were broadcast live over the Internet by the Courtroom 21 Project, sponsored jointly by the William and Mary Law School and the National Center for States Courts. The purpose of the trial was to test the use of high-speed videoconferencing, photo-realistic animations, and a 360 degree dome camera, along with the new court recording system and electronic filing technology.

Courtroom 21 has been used in several real courtroom cases. As many as 500 courtrooms in the United States and Australia have adapted technologies similar to those demonstrated in Courtroom 21. The biggest advantage of the technology-enhanced courtroom is that it promises to lower costs and speed up the overall legal process. Courtroom 21 also provides comprehensive training opportunities for lawyers in any location with modern videoconferencing capabilities.

Source: Gene Stephens, Criminal Justice Editor, The Futurist, Nov./Dec. 2001.

Chapter Three
Paradigms Lost

> The exclusive connection between schools and learning is largely a 20th century phenomenon.

There is a saying among those who observe the change process that the last creature on earth to discover water would be a fish. This is a variation of the old "can't see the forest for the trees" analogy, but the point is the same. Those closest to the situation or problem are often the last to recognize it. This is surely the case in the field of education. Conditions have been changing throughout the history of education, and critics, ranging from university scholars to the man on the street, have been expressing concern. While there is ample evidence that the change process has been a constant part of history, the pace of technological and social change during the 20th century accelerated so rapidly that schools have failed to respond appropriately, resulting in the current crisis in the field of education. The key to understanding the nature of change, and its resulting problems, is the concept of the paradigm.

"Paradigm shift" is a phrase that has been beaten to death in the popular press and used inappropriately often enough to make its meaning almost irrelevant. People can hardly switch breakfast cereals without declaring that they have changed their paradigms. The term "paradigm" actually refers to a major change in the basic manner in which a significant process is perceived and executed: a major change in the way something is done. When a paradigm shifts, all of the previous procedures and rules of operation are called into question and everyone involved in the operation begins anew. Skill and expertise in the old paradigm are of little use since all of the rules have changed. Everyone starts over from zero. For this reason alone paradigm shifts scare the hell out of most people.

History is replete with examples of paradigm shifts that have had the potential to alter the course of human events. Often these events are triggered by technological inventions or political events that significantly influence individuals and societies. This is not to say that every technological advance has led to a paradigm shift. Some, like the invention of the waterwheel in the 6th century and the stirrup in the 8th, had impacts that, while significant, were more localized in nature. Other technological innovations produced dramatic change in far-reaching arenas; the invention of the printing press in 1400s and the linotype machine in1880s are prime examples.

In Europe, the development of the printing press in the 1400s led to the greater production of printed material, the possibility of book ownership by the masses, higher literacy rates, translation of important texts into the language of the people, and eventually a major religious upheaval and scientific revolution. Likewise, the American invention of the linotype machine enabled the masses to access even more printed material, brought the cost of newspapers down to one cent, and doubled the number of newspapers and magazines. An interesting byproduct of this media expansion was the effect it exerted on the American national consciousness by linking the various regions of the country with common influences.

The development of the steam engine and steam locomotive in the early 1800s had a similar effect on transportation. Prior to this time the quickest form of human transportation was a fast horse. This speed factor had remained constant since the first use of horses by ancient civilizations. Steam power revolutionized the field of transportation and shifted the paradigm for human mobility. While the above mentioned events were significant and had a dramatic impact on the environments in which they occurred, they pale in comparison to the quantity and magnitude of the changes that took place during the 20th century.

The Unique Century

The 20th century will be remembered as a time of unprecedented change. And rightly so, for there is no precedent for either the quality or quantity of the technological and social change witnessed during this period. The rapid change that began with the advent of the Industrial Revolution had, by the mid 20th century, reached a pace that biophysicist John Platt described as "incredible squared." These events were so dramatic that Alvin Toffler, who studied the change process, feared that individuals would be unable to cope with rapidly evolving conditions and institutions, and would, as a result, develop a psychological condition that he described as "Future Shock." The sheer volume of technological innovation led socio-economist Kenneth Boulding, to described the 20th century as the mid-point of human history, with as much technological development taking place during this century as had occurred in all the previous centuries of recorded history.

During the 20th century, the inventions of the telegraph, telephone, radio, television, cell phone, and computer shifted the paradigm of communication. The development of the x-ray, antibiotics, the CAT scan, and holistic and preventative medicines altered the paradigm for medical care, and nuclear energy, the atomic and hydrogen bombs, intercontinental ballistic missiles, smart bombs, and stealth bombers revolutionized the practice of warfare. The paradigm for personal transportation was rewritten by the automobile, high-speed train, rapid transit, and the jet airplane. Technological innovations changed the world more between 1900 and 2000 than in all of the previous centuries. As if that were not enough, all indications are that this pace of development will continue to accelerate making the 21st century one of potentially even greater change. Throughout this time of incredible development, only one major institution remained essentially unaltered.

Through eons of social and technological development, the paradigm for education has remained essentially static. The basic format for teaching, teachers speak while students listen, has remained intact since the time of the ancient Egyptians and classical Greeks. Socrates, whose method of teaching by asking questions is still reverently taught in schools of education, would feel right at home in any current secondary school setting! That is not to imply that critics have not warned of the disjuncture between the 20th century educational model and the world it hoped to serve; as early as the late 1800s scholars were making attempts to restructure the American educational paradigm. Scores of essays and countless books have been published lamenting the out-of-date nature of the institution of education. The unique feature they all share is the degree to which they have been ignored. Like the fish, American educators are apparently the last to see what surrounds them.

At least part of this problem lies in the degree to which America has been successful during this time period. There is a common saying: "if it ain't broke don't fix it." People or institutions that are successful are understandably reluctant to change whatever it is that they are doing. For that reason, change almost always comes from the fringes of an organization. People rise to positions of leadership by demonstrating mastery of the operational paradigm. They have achieved a position of dominance and leadership because they have become the most adept at operating whatever system happens to be in place. The last thing they want is to do is restructure the organization, change all of the rules and procedures, and try to once again become the best at managing the new system.

Those on the outside of the organization, or low in its hierarchy or structure, are anxious for change for exactly the same reason. They currently have little or no power and a change in procedure could only help them. Their perspective is very much like the old, classic blues line, "been down so long it looks like up to me." In terms of their position in the organization, they have no direction to go but up. Often it is precisely one's success in a paradigm that makes it difficult to recognize the impending need for change. Past success is at least part of the challenge that America and its educators face at the dawn of the 21st century.

The American Century and the System that Broke It

The 20th century has been described as the "American Century," for it was during this time that America completed its transition from upstart English colony to world power. Early in the century America emerged as an equal participant in world events alongside the traditional powers of Europe, playing a significant role in World War I. After surviving the Great Depression and helping to win World War II, America emerged as one of the world's two great super powers. By the end of the century, the dissolution of the Soviet Union left the United States as the world's leading industrial and military force and only remaining super power. People around the globe looked to America for social, technological, and educational leadership. It is perhaps the greatest irony that, after all of its progress and development, the United States is facing the rigors of the 21st century and the demands of global leadership through reliance on a citizenry armed with an education designed for the conditions of the 19th century.

The current American education system, with its agrarian calendar, evolved at a time when America was making a transition from an agricultural to an industrial economy. Schools were seen as primary tools for the socialization of immigrants and the preparation of workers for America's factories. School buildings were not only architecturally designed to resemble factories, but also operated in a factory-like manner. During the 20th century, America developed from an industrial and agricultural nation to an information and service-based economy. Unfortunately, throughout this remarkable transition, America's educational system remained rooted in the model of the previous century. As management expert Peter Senge states, "The industrial age assembly-line model for education has shaped our schools more than we can imagine – producing generations of 'knowers' not life-long-learners, people beautifully prepared for a world that no longer exists," (Senge, 2001). As the title implies, our purpose in this chapter is to examine the paradigm shifts that have gone unnoticed or have been purposely ignored in the world of education.

During the 20th century, American education systematically failed to adequately respond to a number of major paradigm shifts that had profound effects on its operation. Dramatic research has revolutionized our understanding of the functioning of the human mind. There have been incredible changes in the nature and size of the population to be educated. The American workforce and workplace has gone through at least two major transitions, and the development of electronic technology has revolutionized information management in practically every field save education. Analysis of these paradigms missed goes a long way in explaining the predicament faced by education in the dawn of the 21st century.

When we take a close look at the secondary educational model that was in place during the 20th century, we are shocked to realize that it is based upon a misconception. The model is built on the 19th century idea that the human mind worked like a muscle. The harder it worked, the stronger and larger it became. The educational advocates of this theory were described as "mental disciplinarians." They were firmly committed to the concept that the main function of schooling was the development of the powers of the mind. Process was more important than content. Subjects were rated not by their functional value and use in life, but by their degree of difficulty and thus usefulness in developing the cerebral muscle.

Most famous of the mental disciplinarians was Charles W. Eliot, President of Harvard. In an 1892 address to the National Educational Association, Eliot suggested a complete overhaul of the American educational system from primary school through the university. Eliot stated, "Americans habitually underestimate the capacity of pupils at almost every stage of education." He was firmly committed to the concept that the academic function of the school was paramount.

Eliot was appointed chairman of the famous Committee of Ten, which was commissioned to make recommendations for high school curricular reform. Among the committee's recommendations was the idea that all subjects should be taught to all students in the same exact way. They stated, "every subject which is taught at all in a secondary school should be taught in the same way and to the same extent to every pupil so long as he pursues it." Eliot's influence was also felt in the work of the Committee of Fifteen, which made recommendations for elementary education. This group recommended that "grammar, literature, arithmetic, geography, and history were seen as central subjects for training the mind – and clear separation of those subjects was essential." A few years later, the Carnegie Foundation for the Advancement of Teaching created the still-used Carnegie Unit. Their purpose was to standardize the amount of time spent on each subject of the high school curriculum to aid in the process of college admissions.

From this point forward we had a system of education that purposely fragmented the subjects of the curriculum, avoiding any connections between and among the subjects taught. Each subject was taught in the same size classroom, with the same number of students, for the exact same length of time. The value of a given subject was not measured in terms of its functional use, but rather by its degree of difficulty, and therefore its potential for developing the cerebral muscle. Greater prestige was accorded to both teachers and students of Latin grammar than to practitioners of physical education due to the perceived degree of difficulty associated with the subjects. Scant attention was paid to the long-term applicability of the subject matter. Forget the fact that a sound Health/P.E. curriculum could lead to a longer, healthier, and more comfortable lifestyle; Latin was seen as more valuable because it was considered to be more demanding – not to mention that P.E. activities committed the unpardonable sin of appearing fun. There was no place for laxity or fun in the "no pain, no gain" model of cerebral muscular growth.

A sure-fire way to start a brawl in a faculty room is to ask the teachers to rank order the importance of the subjects of the curriculum. Understandably, every teacher believes that his or her subject is the lynchpin of the academic universe. Yet in a world of exponential knowledge growth, diminishing financial resources, and a set-in-stone academic calendar, some sort of ranked priorities among the subjects should be discussed. Few could argue with the idea that every subject need not be taught in the same sized room, with the same number of students, for the same amount of time, and yet the only significant variation of this theme in evidence is the block schedule (in which classes meet for longer periods of time for fewer days per week). For some subjects, such as the laboratory sciences, this is a welcome change. A longer class period allows the instructor sufficient time to setup and breakdown lab equipment and for the students to get totally immersed in the activity. For other class activities it is a hindrance. Classes such as creative writing, which do not need to meet with an instructor in a formal setting to actually do their work, find the block schedule to be more of what they don't need: class time. The fact that there are differences between and among subject areas is obvious. We can no longer let the threat of disagreement prevent us from addressing this critical subject.

The concept of the mind as a muscle would be the stuff of high humor were it not connected with episodes of pseudo-scientific, racist research and dysfunctional educational outcomes. In the former case, researchers involved in the study of intelligence developed the concept of craniology, which centered on the measurement of the cranial capacity of deceased members of various ethnic and social groups in hopes of proving that certain races and societal factions were more intelligent than others. The proof of greater intelligence, they believed, would be evidenced by greater cranial capacity. Since the theory was flawed to begin with, the research yielded inconclusive data. Causal links could not be established between brain size and intelligence in either ethnic or social groups. The results in some cases were rather comical, with researchers finding that the brains of noted scholars were measurably smaller than the brains of executed criminals. In addition, no distinct differences could be found between the various ethnic groups studied. Undeterred, the researchers "proved" their theory, in some cases by falsifying data.

In education, this scientific nonsense left us with a curriculum based on an inaccurate picture of the nature of intelligence and how people learn. Had the craniologists been correct, intelligence testing would have been as simple as measuring hat sizes! As it turned out, we were saddled, throughout the 20th century, with an educational paradigm that disregarded the differences between students' learning abilities and learning styles. The unique nature of the various subject areas, along with time requirements, facility needs, and class-size mandates, were completely and systematically ignored. As we enter the third millennium, we are faced with a rapidly changing world that demands appropriate strategies to insure educational success. A curriculum based on classic misconceptions from the 19th century will not well serve the educational demands of the 21st.

In addition to misunderstanding the paradigm of the human mind, educators also misjudged the nature of the population to be served. The roots of American education lie in religious training and practice. The Puritans who landed at Plymouth were originally English Calvinists who wanted to change or purify the Anglican Church. The ideals of the Reformation did not go far enough for Puritans who left England seeking greater religious freedom. They strongly believed in Luther's doctrine of the "priesthood of all believers" and deemed it necessity for children to learn to read the Scriptures. Early educational efforts were intended to give the common man the ability to read the Bible in his native language.

The Pilgrims considered education to be a parental responsibility, but as early as 1642, the General Court of Massachusetts came to believe that many parents were failing in this obligation. In 1647, the General Court passed the famous Old Deluder Satan Act, which required that every town establish a school. The curriculum in these early schools centered on the three "R's," religion, reading, and writing, and was almost entirely religious in nature. The purpose of education was salvation as well as preparation for life.

While the early establishment of colonial schools appeared to represent an auspicious start for American education, there was significant opposition to the concept in some areas. The theory of public elementary education for every child found wide acceptance in areas of frontier America; however the raising of tax money to support the schools often met with a great deal of opposition. Sound familiar? Many newspapers came out against the raising of taxes to support schools. Progress in the area of school development was hindered by the tradition that the education of children was primarily the responsibility of parents and secondarily that of the church. Eventually these prejudices against public schools were overcome, and by 1850, 45 percent of the nation's children attended elementary schools. The prospect of high school education was a different matter.

Early secondary education consisted of Latin grammar schools, academies, and high schools. Latin grammar schools were designed to serve the needs of the college-bound elite, and, since high tuition was charged, were available only to students of means. "Female seminaries," girls' academies, offered a less rigorous academic curriculum, including courses in needlework and embroidery. Boys' and girls' academies flourished between 1750 and 1850, with an estimated 6,000 schools serving over 260,000 students. Admittance, once again, was available only to those who could afford the tuition.

The first free secondary school was the English Classical School for Boys in Boston, established in 1821. Later it was renamed the English High School which was the first time that term was used. The academies, as well as the taxpayers, bitterly opposed the establishment of public high schools. It took the 1874 Kalamazoo Case for the Michigan Supreme Court to finally confirm the right of a state to establish public education at the secondary level at public expense. In 1900, there were 6,000 public high schools with 519,000 students. Ten percent of all American youth attended high school by 1900. The turn of the century also marked a dramatic change in who was to attend secondary education.

Change in the Work Place and Education Paradigms

At the beginning of the 20th century, America was well along in the process of making the transition from an agricultural to industrial society. The turn of the century was characterized by a tremendous increase in industrial growth, especially in the northern and eastern states. This post Civil War growth of industry was changing America from an agricultural society into a developing industrial power.

The first U.S. Census, in 1790, had indicated that there were only four million Americans, and that 90 percent of them lived on small self-sufficient farms. During this same period, the Industrial Revolution was already sweeping England. America's somewhat slower entry into the Industrial Revolution was aided by businessmen such as Francis Lowell, who built mills that transformed the pioneer economy of the New England area. By employing women and children in his mills, he changed the social fabric as well. Inventor Cyrus McCormick developed the reaper in the 1830s and freed thousands of workers from the farm to find work in the growing number of factories and mills.

Many of these mill and factory workers were young children. The involvement of children in the workforce goes back to the time of the Puritans. Children often worked beside their parents in the fields and in cottage industries. Often children were apprenticed at an early age to craftsmen for the purpose of learning a trade in a longstanding tradition dating to the craft guilds of medieval Europe. In the agricultural and cottage industry economy that characterized America from colonial settlement to the rise of industrialism in the 19th century, child labor was thought to be a part of the educational process that prepared youth for productive lives.

With the 19th century advent of major mining enterprises and factory production, the nature of child labor underwent a radical transformation. The emphasis shifted from preparing children for productive lives to providing mine and factory owners with a pool of cheap, unskilled, and docile workers. In 1832, one-third of the nation's factory workforce was made up of children who worked seventy-two hours per week under appalling conditions for as little as eleven cents per day.

By 1900, the use of children in mines, factories, and sweatshops had become a national scandal. The turn of the century census revealed that more than 1.7 million children between the ages of ten and fifteen were employed in the workforce. Thousands under the age of twelve worked in mines; thousands more worked in textile mills and factories. Some children as young as four years old worked with their immigrant parents eking out a living in the sweatshops of Boston and New York. This scandal finally prompted labor leaders and social reformers to pressure Congress, during the Wilson administration, to force through federal legislation limiting child labor. While it took several decades of legislation and a number of Supreme Court decisions to resolve the issue of child labor, the paradigm of childhood had begun to shift.

With the advent of child-labor awareness, and subsequent laws freeing children from the workplace, new institutions were developed to deal with this segment of the population. Kindergartens, orphanages, reform schools, fresh air camps, humane societies, and boys' and girls' clubs were established to deal with children.

One older institution, the American high school, was also used to occupy the time of these individuals no longer deemed suitable for the workplace. Universal education was extended to the secondary level, with record numbers of students attending high schools. During the early decades of the 20th century, high schools doubled in enrollment every ten years. By 1900, public secondary schools were almost all coeducational, with more than half of the student body comprised of young women. The shift in the workforce paradigm changed the nature of public education. The lack of a purposeful shift in the curriculum represented a problem in the organization of these newly populated schools.

The purpose of the early academies and high schools had been to provide college preparation for young men of means. The new public secondary schools served a significantly different student-body. Not only were the schools coeducational, but, in 1900, only 10 percent of the graduates expected to enter college. Most high schools offered both a traditional (college prep) and practical (employment after graduation) program, but the emphasis was clearly placed on the college preparatory curriculum. This "classical" course of study was taken by the majority of youngsters, in spite of the fact that it did not directly address the needs of 90 percent of them! From its beginnings, the American comprehensive high school missed the needs of the majority of its student population.

There is evidence that this irony was noted by educators of the day. As early as 1893, members of the Committee of Ten indicated that they did not view the function of high school as solely college preparatory. They noted, "The secondary schools of the United States, taken as a whole, do not exist for the purpose of preparing boys and girls for colleges. Only an insignificant percentage of the graduates of these schools go to colleges or scientific schools." Despite this revelation, the committee recommended that all subjects be taught to all students in the same way – regardless of program!

Even early in the century, this approach to education elicited outrage from scholars such as G. Stanley Hall, who attacked the idea in his 1904 book *Adolescence*. Hall believed that the "one size fits all" approach to education ignored large numbers of students who needed very different programs and methods of instruction. Perhaps the most amazing irony is the fact that nearly a century later, when current high school principals are asked to give evidence of the quality of their schools academic programs, they routinely point to the percentage of their graduates that go on to higher education! After more than a century, American high schools are still operating on a paradigm that is designed to serve the needs of a minority of students!

As if the general confusion about its purpose was not enough, early high schools compounded the issue by making their buildings resemble and operate like factories. In 1903, Henry Ford founded the Ford Motor Company, where (in 1913) he pioneered a new method of industrial production: the assembly line. In this new model of manufacturing efficiency, the workers stayed in one location while their products came to them for assembly and adjustment. The day started and ended with the sounding of a bell or horn, and lunch and rest breaks were announced by the same method. The assembly line was a revolutionary change in the industrial world and was considered a model of efficiency. Amazingly, educators, whose goal was to provide every student with a college preparatory education, adopted the same model for the newly expanded secondary schools.

In the new secondary school, teachers stayed in one location, their classroom, while a steady stream of students moved by for instruction. The school day started and ended with the sound of a bell, and the same signal announced the arrival of the lunch break. Bells also indicated the beginning and ending of each work period, during which a uniform number of students worked with a teacher for a uniform number of minutes, regardless of the nature or complexity of the subject or activity. Leading curriculum writers of the day, such as Franklin Bobbitt, spoke of schools in terms of industrial productivity, describing the transformation of the raw material (the student) into the finished product (the model adult). However, there is little indication that the irony of using a factory paradigm of operation for the purpose of preparing students for college was widely recognized. As if this were not enough, this organizational oddity carried over into the structure of the school's calendar year.

In early days of non-mechanized agriculture, children were an essential resource in the operation of the family farm. Large numbers of children were considered an asset in that they provided a captive pool of manual labor for their families. Because of the importance of this labor force, school schedules were designed to free students to help their parents during the labor-intensive times of the agricultural year, namely late spring through early fall. As the technical innovations of the 1800s (such as the previously mentioned McCormick reaper) became widespread, the paradigm for agriculture began to shift. Much of the intense manual labor performed by humans and animals was being taken over by machines. Family farms were slowly giving way to larger corporate agricultural operations. Increasing numbers of farm families were moving to cities to work in the growing ranks of industry.

By the turn of the 20th century, America was well on its way to becoming primarily an industrial nation. The process may have been gradual, but the result was undeniable. Between 1790 and 1970 (180 years), the demographic make-up of the country had completely reversed! In 1790, U.S. Marshals on horseback took the first Federal Census and counted 3.9 million Americans, spread evenly among the states. All but 5 percent of the population was living on farms. By 1970, the population was 208.2 million, with fifty-nine persons per square mile. Almost three-quarters of these people lived in cities and urban areas and only 5 percent lived on farms.

America was no longer a country of farmers; the age of industry had arrived. And yet, at the end of the 20th century, our schools still operate on a calendar designed to meet the needs of an agricultural age long past. While it seems obvious that no functional multi-billion dollar enterprise could expect to be successful employing a paradigm of operation that requires it to cease productivity 25 percent of the time, education has tenaciously clung to this pattern. As we race forward in the post-industrial world and look to our educational system with its agrarian time model, do we really have to wonder why it is not maximally efficient? Yet again we operate within a paradigm of the past.

Bad Scope, Bad Sequence

Not only is the school calendar questionably functional, the paradigm for education in terms of scope is also a cause for concern. There are at least two parts of the present educational paradigm that are dysfunctional in terms of scope and duration. The first concerns the length of time allocated for public education and the second deals with the overall timeframe for educating an individual.

For most of the 20th century, American public education consisted of a Kindergarten through senior high school experience that exposed students to approximately fifteen thousand hours of instructional time. During that same timeframe what scholars describe as the "body of human knowledge" (everything that we as intelligent humans know), has doubled a countless number of times. The characteristics of the world at the end of the 20th century are exponentially different than they were at the beginning. Socio-economist Kenneth Boulding expressed this phenomenon well when he asserted, "The world of today…is as different from the world in which I was born as that world was from Julius Caesar's. I was born in the middle of human history, to date, roughly. Almost as much has happened since I was born as happened before" (1962). As frightening as the implications of this statement may be, there are many that choose to ignore them. As Alvin Toffler stated in *Future Shock*, "The disturbing fact is that the vast majority of people, including educated and otherwise sophisticated people, find the idea of change so threatening that they attempt to deny its existence." He goes on to point out that "Millions sleepwalk their way through their lives as if nothing had changed since the 1930s and as if nothing ever will" (1970). Those millions include public school educators who have stayed with a consistent fifteen thousand hour schedule through a century of tumultuous change.

It isn't as though the issue of change did not occur to anyone in the educational community. In 1935, the National Education Association established the Educational Policy Commission for the purpose of articulating a national policy for education. While the report was in many ways seriously out of date, describing model curricula for only two distinct types of American cities ("Farmville" and "American City"), it did strongly recommend the innovative concept of educating all children and youth from the ages of three through twenty. Their model featured a public nursery school, followed by a six-year elementary school experience, and finally an eight-year high school, which would include Grades 13 and 14. Unfortunately there is little evidence to suggest that these recommendations were taken seriously enough to be implemented. Education was left with a rapidly changing world and a static model of educational delivery. There were only two real possibilities for the outcome: Either teachers would have to present materials at a much more rapid rate during those traditional fifteen thousand hours, or much of the newly developed information made available during the century was going to be missed. We know what happened!

The second issue concerns the concept of the scope of education. There was a time when the concept of "getting one's education" had a degree of validity. In the pre-industrial world of crafts and craftsmanship, it was possible to learn a trade, terminate your education, and spend the rest of your life practicing that set of skills. In early colonial times, silversmiths like Paul Revere could expect, as an apprentice, to learn the trade of working with silver, have their masterpiece evaluated as evidence of their competency, and be accepted into the guild of master craftsmen. Changes in most fields of endeavor were either nonexistent, or so insignificant that the concept of continuing education or training was both unnecessary and unheard of. It was in this world that the levels of education were established. Students progressed through elementary school, high school, and eventually college. The final or highest degree available was referred to as the "terminal degree."

It still is today. Despite the indication that scholars as early as John Dewey viewed education, not as preparation for life but an inseparable and on-going part of life, many others still tragically view education as a finite process. The tragedy lies in the fact that in a world of exponential change, in which some estimate that the body of human knowledge doubles every thirteen months, those who choose to terminate their educational process, in effect, create their own blueprint for obsolescence. Unless the pace of change was to suddenly slow, the only effective strategy for survival must, of necessity, include a plan for continual education and life-long-learning. Rather than talking in terms of a K-12 curriculum, educators should be meeting the demands of the new millennium with a cradle-to-grave model.

Does Spelling Count In This Class?

Yet another feature of 20th century schools that represents a paradigm problem is the previously mentioned uniformity and isolation of the subject areas. Shortly after the Committee of Ten was commissioned by the NEA to make recommendations regarding the organization of secondary education, the Committee of Fifteen was charged with the same mission for the elementary level. Among the committee's more interesting recommendations were two that fly in the face of modern pedagogical understanding. The first was that the scientific method of teaching science should not be used with elementary students. The view of the committee was that students of this age lacked the mental capacity to benefit from the discovery process (learning by doing) and should be taught through teacher lectures (the least interactive of delivery methods). The second pearl of wisdom offered by this group was that grammar, literature, arithmetic, geography, and history should be seen as the central subjects for the training of the mind and therefore a clear separation of the subjects was essential. Again the mind was viewed as a cerebral muscle and the relationship between and among the subject areas was of no consequence. The net effect of this committee's work was to sustain a fragmented and subject-centered approach to curriculum development.

It is this planned fragmentation of the curriculum that leads to sadly comical exchanges between students and their teachers. As an example: A science teacher returns a paper to a student with the observation that almost every third word is misspelled. The student offers the defense that this is a science class and that spelling should not count as a part of a science grade. As sad and silly as this scenario may sound, it is the product of years of students being told that making connections between subjects is inappropriate. It is entirely possible that this same student at some point asked a science or mathematics teacher a grammar or spelling-related question only to be told to "go ask your English teacher!"

It is ironic that even early in the 20th century, when the NEA committees were meeting, scholars were trying to warn of the dangers of a fragmented approach. As Francis W. Parker pointed out in 1894, "self-contained subjects prevent children from seeing beyond a limited mental horizon." In 1964, Marshall McLuhan stated, "In education the conventional division of the curriculum into subjects is already as outdated as the medieval trivium and quadrivium after the Renaissance. Any subject taken in depth at once relates to other subjects … continued in their present patterns of fragmented unrelation, our school curricula will ensure a citizenry unable to understand the cybernated world in which they live."

As we begin the 21st century, we are well aware that the mind is not a muscle and that effective comprehension and appropriate application of educational materials requires a functional understanding of the relationships among and between the subjects of the curriculum. The paradigm of a fragmented curriculum is yet another ghost from the past.

The Paradigm of School as a Place

One of the informal but enduring concepts in the field of education has been the connection between schools and learning. When asked where they go to be educated, most people today, without hesitation, would respond, "school of course!" Yet this was not always the case.

The tradition in America, as late as the 19th century, was that children should be educated first by their parents and second by the church (Pulliam, 1987). There was a time in American history when it was customary to teach children to read and write before sending them to school! For some social and ethnic groups, education was not considered primarily the responsibility of the state (Pulliam). Catholic doctrine traditionally insisted that the primary responsibility for education rested with the parents and the Church. The state, they believed, should have only a secondary role in education. The exclusive connection between schools and learning is largely a 20th century phenomenon.

While the main function of 20th century schools has been the process of education, they have had far less of a monopoly on that function than they would like to imagine. The home, churches, clubs, teams, and civic and social organizations are all very much in the business of educating the populace. Quite often the subject matter covered by these institutions is remarkably similar to that of the public schools. In the areas of social, moral, and character education, there is a surprising amount of duplication of effort, and yet the amount of coordination between these civic, religious, and educational groups is practically nonexistent. Most American public schools are so insular in nature that they consider a strong, active program of parent and teacher interaction to be a significant innovation. The flurry of excitement in the business world centered on the promise and potential of networking has been ignored in the realm of American schools. Public education also lags behind business and industry in the area of worker incentives.

The Incentive Paradigm

In the realm of business and management, the 20th century represented the high water mark in terms of research in the field of worker motivation. Theoretical approaches to worker motivation by scholars such as McGregor, Maslow, Herzberg, Ouchi, Peters and Waterman, Demmings, Drucker, and Senge added new insight to the field of supervision. While their approaches varied widely, they did converge on the basic premise that the harder and more efficiently a person worked, the more successful that person tended to become. This was a variation on the old folk saying, "The harder you work, the luckier you get." The basic concept is difficult to argue with – except in the field of education.

American elementary and secondary schools have created an incentive system that defies the logic of management. Teachers are not rewarded for working harder; they are rewarded for continuing education and aging. Most school district contracts feature a grid consisting of steps and lanes that determine where a teacher fits within the district's negotiated pay schedule. Teachers move across the schedules lanes by meeting the requirements for earned units of continuing education. After earning a required number of additional college credits, the teacher qualifies for the next lane on the pay schedule. To move to the next step on the schedule, the teacher must gain one more year of experience. There are two interesting assumptions that serve as the justification for this process.

The rationale for paying teachers more money for earned credits of continuing education is based on the assumption that the more knowledgeable the teacher is, the more skillful he or she will become in the classroom. In theory, greater expertise in a subject area should lead to greater competency as an instructor. The problem lies in the fact that while some districts monitor this process closely and only allow credit for courses that will clearly improve the teacher's skills as an instructor or classroom manager, many districts give the same credit value to coaching clinics, academically questionable workshop activities, travel experiences, and attendance at state and local teachers conferences. It takes a mighty leap of faith to envision how some of these activities could possibly improve teacher efficiency to the level that would warrant increasing salary. Understanding movement across the steps takes an even greater leap.

The assumption behind the steps on the pay schedule is that additional years of experience make a person a better and more skillful teacher. In some cases this is undoubtedly true. In others it is meaningless. Dedicated teachers constantly hone their skills and work to improve their craft with each year of experience. Others start their teaching experience with a year of bumbling incompetence and then replicate this experience twenty-nine more times during a thirty year career. Amazingly, each of these teachers could be in exactly the same place on the pay schedule! The question is often posed as to why we do not have better teachers in our nation's schools. The more appropriate question might be why, given the incentive system we employ, do we have any competent teachers at all? The difference between an award-winning teacher and a blazing incompetent is indistinguishable in terms of compensation. It is clearly intrinsic motivation that prompts the exemplary teacher to soldier on in the presence of this system.

Where Have All the Teachers Gone?

Among the plethora of issues threatening the continued existence of schools is the question of staffing. Will schools be able to find teachers and administrators? Will a critical teacher shortage herald the end of the places we call schools? When considering this question, a good starting point is teacher backgrounds. Where have teachers come from?

Conventional wisdom tells us that teachers are "solidly middle class." As is so often the case, generalizations like this are oversimplifications. Teachers have and do come from a variety of social and economic backgrounds. Until the early 20th century, urban teachers came from middle-class backgrounds, while rural teachers had farming and working-class roots. As the nation became more industrialized, the nature of the workforce changed. Some states passed compulsory attendance statutes, while others began to enforce existing laws. The demand for teachers increased and so did the opportunities for more diverse social groups. As Americans left the farms and moved to industrial jobs in the cities, there was a corresponding decline in the number of teachers who came from agricultural backgrounds. A study conducted prior to World War II indicated that 38 percent of teachers came from farming backgrounds (Greenhoe, 1941). By 1986, a National Education Association survey indicated that only 13 percent of teachers came from farming families, and further, teachers came from all classes of American society (N.E.A., 1987, p. 162). While the ranks of the teaching profession represented the entire cross-section of

American life, the largest segment of teachers came from lower middle-class or upper lower-class backgrounds. The great unifying factor, late in the 20th century, was that teachers as a group were upwardly mobile. The teaching profession represented a popular career-ladder route to a type of white-collar work associated with middle-class life. According to Dan Lortie, "Teaching is clearly white-collar, middle-class work and as such offers upward mobility for people who grew up in blue-collar or lower-class families" (1975). As of 1986, 38 percent of teacher's fathers were not high school graduates (N.E.A., 1987).

Beyond upward-mobility, Lortie's research indicated that people were also attracted to teaching by what they perceived as the prestige of the profession: good income relative to their working-class backgrounds, and job security. The previously mentioned N.E.A. study indicated that there were three primary motivations for people to enter the teaching field. These three, somewhat idealistic motivations were: a desire to work with young people, an interest in the subject matter to be taught, and a perception that education is of value to society.

Also of interest were the reasons that teachers gave for remaining in the field. When asked why they stayed in teaching, the three primary motives were still evident, along with the addition of long summer vacations, job security, and the need for a second family income. Lortie found two other reasons for becoming teachers: the continuation motive, and the blocked-aspirations motive.

For some people, the experience of going to school as a student was so intensely satisfying that they had a strong desire to perpetuate this positive environment. Individuals who had great success as athletes found coaching to be a means of continuing that experience. Students who had great success in a particular academic subject continued the feeling by becoming teachers in that area. For many, teaching was a means to capitalize on early success in life.

Education could also be a fallback profession after a primary career choice did not work out. For individuals who had really wanted to be actors, athletes, or artists but couldn't generate a living in these fields, teaching allowed them to become drama teachers, coaches, and art teachers, thus remaining connected to their area of interest. A student unable to gain entrance to, or remain in, medical school might choose teaching biology as a way to work in a related field. A student who was unsuccessful in an engineering program could feel comfortable teaching high school mathematics or physics. Education may also provide a place to work until such time as a person is discovered and able to flourish in a primary field. For example, across the country, English departments are peppered with English teachers waiting for their first successful novel or play to be published.

A third group, motivated by blocked-aspirations is made up of educators who have, for a variety of reasons, become disillusioned with another profession. In fifteen years of teaching educational leadership courses, one of the authors has advised six individuals who had left the practice of law to become teachers or administrators. The desire to work in a more ethical and satisfying environment was the rationale expressed in all six cases.

Whatever their reason for becoming teachers, historically, people have not remained in the field for long. A study by Herbert Walberg, in 1970 indicated that the average career expectancy for teachers was about two years (Walberg, 1970). Since the time of this study, the average for teaching careers has become longer, but the cause of this shift has little to do with teachers or education. Nearly a decade of double-digit inflation following the end of the war in Vietnam prompted many teachers to remain in the field. In tough economic times the prospect of leaving a secure teaching job was more of a risk than most teachers were willing or able to take. This trend has continued into the new millennium with uncertain economic conditions, prompting many teachers of retirement age to remain on the job.

The phenomenon of teacher dissatisfaction is hardly a recent development. Surveys in 1966 indicated that 53 percent of teachers would certainly choose to become teachers again. By the mid 1980s that number had dropped to 23 percent (Teacher Education Reports, 1985). A subsequent Harris Poll indicated that, of a national sample of teachers, 51 percent had considered leaving the profession and 27 percent indicated that they would likely leave teaching within the next five years. Perhaps most shocking was the finding that the very best teachers (individuals who had won awards for teaching) were the most likely to indicate an intention to leave the classroom. By 1997, 34 percent of a national sample of practicing teachers indicated that they were not sure that they would choose teaching as a career given the opportunity to go back and begin again. The majority of this group stated that, given the present system of evaluation and rewards, they considered it a waste of time to do their best as a teacher (National Center for Educational Statistics, 1997). Throughout this time period, the most often cited reasons for disenchantment with the teaching profession were low salaries and limited career opportunities.

The tale of teacher compensation has been a roller coaster ride for much of the second half of the 20th century. At the end of World War II, American teachers earned considerably less than the average worker. As a part of the national response to the launching of the Russian satellite Sputnik, significant amounts of funding were pumped into education, and teachers' salaries went up. According to the U.S. Department of Education (1986), by the 1971-72 school year, the $10,000 salary of the average teacher had surpassed the earnings of the average American worker ($8,334). Then the bottom fell out of the American economy. The recession following the end of the war in Vietnam resulted in the previously mentioned eight years of double-digit inflation. Between 1971 and 1984 the average salary for teachers rose from $10,000 to $22,877, but in reality, teachers lost ground. Taking into account inflation, the purchasing power of teachers declined by $2,251 (U.S. Dept. of Education, 1986). Teacher's salaries continued to go up, while their real buying power dropped. At the same time, other professions began to gain ground. By 1986, the national average salary for teachers had reached $24,559. The national average for those in other professions with four years of college was $32,216. Teachers were earning over $7,000 less than other American workers with a four-year college education (National Center for Educational Information, 1986). The ravages of inflation continued to take a toll on the field of education.

The second area most often cited by dissatisfied teachers is the limited opportunity for advancement. As we have mentioned before, education, as a profession, is woefully lacking in the area of career incentives. In teaching there is little or no financial recognition and thus compensation for excellent performance. A teacher's salary will progress along a negotiated scale in fixed steps, regardless of effort or accomplishment. Inept teachers traverse the salary scale at the exact same pace as the excellent ones. A teacher can graduate from college, serve in the classroom for forty years, and retire making a salary that is less than twice the amount earned by a new teacher. This represents a pay differential that is significantly lower than those found in private-sector professions. Teachers are paid less than other college graduates at the beginning of their careers and continue to fall further and further behind throughout the course of their careers (Webb and Sherman, 1989). The picture is no brighter for the most ambitious teachers.

One of the great ironies of education is the fact that the only way to get ahead in the field of teaching is to leave it. Individuals who want to advance in the field of education leave teaching and become administrators. The ultimate reward for demonstrating excellence in teaching is to become an administrator who will seldom, if ever, have the opportunity to teach. Education offers few formal rewards for excellent performance. As Ernest Boyer noted, "The lack of opportunity for advancement in teaching is in sharp contrast to other professions, where outstanding performance is rewarded" (1983). As if the real conditions for education and educators have not been challenging enough, the last half of the 20th century featured a thorough thrashing of the public's image of the profession and its practitioners.

There was a time in the not-too-distant past when teaching was considered to be an honorable way to make a living. Educational historian, Diane Ravitch stated, "fifty years ago . . . there was an almost automatic respect for the teacher. The teacher was the most educated person in the community. That's no longer the case. Teachers find themselves perhaps the lowest ranking of all professions. [They] find themselves struggling for the respect of the communities, struggling for the respect of the parents, and struggling for the respect of the students" (quoted in Frady, 1985). American society has blamed teachers and education for every form of social ill during the last fifty years, radically altering the previous feeling of respect. As if there was not already a sufficient array of real concerns in the field of education, beginning in the 1950s, schools were blamed for issues as diverse as America's slow start in the space race (Sputnik) to endangering the safety of the entire nation (A Nation At Risk). The result has been an interesting disjuncture between the way educators and the rest of the general public view the profession. As early as the mid 1980s, the Gallup Poll of teacher's attitudes indicated that "Teachers rate their contributions to society the *highest* of twelve professions, including physicians, clergy, business executives, and lawyers. But they also feel that their status is the *lowest* of all these professions" (1984).

Confusing as this is, there is not only a seeming disagreement between poll findings, but striking disparities within the same research findings. Throughout the series of Gallup Polls measuring the American's attitudes toward public schools (the 2003 edition was poll number thirty-five) there is a contradiction between what Americans think of the educational system as a whole and how they perceive their local schools. Americans routinely report that they are dissatisfied with U.S. education in general, but quite happy with the schools their children attend. Teachers are somehow expected to make sense of this confusing message.

The maddening situations that educators face will inevitably have a disastrous effect on the future recruitment of teachers. A series of questions come to mind concerning this issue. How many intelligent young people are going to rush to serve in a profession that has become the standard whipping post for society and its politicians? How many decades of public criticism must education endure before potential teachers begin to shun teaching? Will education continue to represent a career ladder for individuals aspiring toward white-collar, middle-class life if it continues to offer less compensation than other jobs requiring a four-year college education and continues to sink in terms of public perception? Can teaching survive when its most ambitious practitioners are forced to leave teaching for administration, or leave education for fields offering better financial opportunities? Can any profession prosper when its peak-performers, its award-winning teachers, are the most likely people to leave? The answers are clearly and collectively "no!" Schools, due to their dysfunctional incentive paradigm, will soon be asking, "Where have all the teachers gone?"

Of course, there is a follow up question schools should be asking, since they are in the same boat. The motivation paradigm for schools is no better than that for teachers. Schools are not rewarded for educating students either quickly or efficiently. They are rewarded for having them in attendance. Average Daily Attendance, or Average Number Belonging totals are the basis for a district's support of a school. School funding is based on the number of occupied seats. There is a major incentive to keep students on the school's rolls as long as possible, regardless of achievement or behavior. Schools often tolerate students who have enthusiastically demonstrated their lack of interest in learning because the schools can't afford to lose the support money that would follow those students out the door. Once again, is there any other multi-billion dollar industry that could honestly expect to prosper with similar forms of worker and institutional incentives in place? As if all of these missed paradigm shifts, representing potential dangers to educators and the field of education were not enough, there is one catastrophic shift that will surly rewrite the paradigm for education during this latest century.

The Unrecognized Revolution

Until 1948, electronic devices such as the radio, television, and even the very early computer relied on vacuum tubes to transmit electronic current impulses. While they worked quite well, the tubes were relatively large, quite fragile, and prone to failure. Tubes were expensive, required a warm-up period, consumed a great deal of energy, and were short-lived under the best of conditions. In 1948, three physicists working for Bell Laboratories discovered a new kind of crystal that was a "semiconductor" of electricity and led to the invention of the transistor. This technological development changed the second half of the 20th century by making is possible to build an incredible variety of portable and dependable electronic devices. Computers that originally filled a room with their tubes and wires were eventually reduced to the size of a device that could rest comfortably on a table or desk. Radios, once the size of a toaster, could now be easily put in a shirt pocket.

As research continued, transistors were made smaller and smaller, until, by 1960, it was possible to etch transistors into tiny thin wafers of silicon called chips. Subsequent developments made it possible to etch millions of microscopic transistors into a single one-inch square chip, allowing the manufacture of very powerful and inexpensive devices such as desktop computers, aircraft guidance systems, and portable cellular telephones.

At the end of this decade of electronic innovation, the U.S. Department of Defense created the Advanced Research Projects Agency Network (ARPANET) for the purpose of allowing organizations involved in defense-related research to communicate through a secure network in the event of an outside attack. The net had a common addressing system and communications protocol called the Transmission Control Protocol/Internet Protocol (TCP/IP). While designed for the use of defense-related research, academics and researchers in other fields began to use the computerized network. At approximately the same time, the National Science Foundation created a similar and parallel network called NSFNet. Eventually the National Science Foundation adopted much of the TCP/IP technology from ARPANET and established a wider network that had the capacity to handle a greater amount of traffic. In 1983, the National Science Foundation called its new network the "Internet" which grew rapidly, far beyond its original academic origins. By 1995, the Internet connected more than two million computers in over one hundred countries. Twenty-five million users were able to log on to what U.S. Vice President Al Gore called the "information highway."

The key to the individual's ability to use this groundbreaking technology was the advent of the personal computer. An article in the magazine *Popular Electronics* in 1975 stated: "The era of the computer in every home – a favorite topic among science-fiction writers – has arrived." Their reference was to the Altair 8800, which was a build-it-yourself construction project outlined in an electronics magazine. Crude as the Altair is by today's standards, it proved to be far more popular than anyone had imagined, and, by 1977, new companies such as Apple and Commodore were being founded to produce more sophisticated personal computers. Soon other established electronics companies like Radio Shack and Heath got into this lucrative "niche market."

Traditional computer companies were notably slow to enter the personal computer marketplace. As early as 1943, IBM chairman, Thomas J. Watson, had stated: "I think there is a world market for about five computers" (Barker 1992). As late as 1977, Ken Olsen, President of Digital, added: "There is no reason for any individual to have a computer in their home" (Barker). Finally in 1981, IBM brought out its first personal home computer, the "PC" and the computer revolution began. Almost overnight, the paradigm for access and dispersal of information, the mainstay of education, had shifted. Unfortunately most educators managed to miss the main point.

The Joy of Camel Ownership

It is not our purpose to imply that educators did not embrace the use of computers in their school settings. The problem is the way in which these new devices were used. The fact is that educators took to the idea of computers in schools with all of the enthusiasm of an alcoholic in a brewery. They had a hunch that computers were important and that having them would seem prestigious, however, beyond that, most educators had no idea what to do with the machines. It is like the story of the man who wins a camel in a raffle at the county fair and is wildly enthusiastic about winning until he realizes that now he owns a camel.

Some schools bought simple Radio Shack computers and set about teaching students how to program them. Others used them as overpriced typewriters. For many schools and their computer illiterate teachers and administrators, simply having the machines was of much greater importance than any conceivable student usage. Apple and other computer companies facilitated the acquisition process with special programs like *Apple For A Teacher*. The race was on! Nationwide educators believed that they were preparing their students for the world of computer literacy and the age of information. By ignoring or simply misunderstanding the academic potential of technology, education missed this critical paradigm shift in at least two ways. Education was missing the boat in terms of both quantity and quality.

The claim that schools were acquiring technology was a good intention that, in application, varied widely from school to school and district to district. In some cases it meant that the school had a computer; in others it meant that there was a comprehensive technology education program with a low student to computer ratio. Yet, in the best of situations, the gap between what schools were doing to prepare students to operate in the "real world" and what "real world" institutions were doing in terms of technology was enormous. According to a 1988 study by the U.S. Congress's Office of Technology Assessment, education spent less on the purchase of technology than any other major industry in the country. Industries' average expenditure for capital investment per job was $50,000 of capital investment, with some high tech companies spending up to $300,000 or more in technology for each worker. The average for education was $1,000 per employee. The second part of the paradigm problem was in the area of quality.

The traditional role of the teacher was to dispense information, and the classic educational model was the "sage on the stage" who delivered material in the time-honored lecture format and later tested the students' ability to comprehend by asking them to regurgitate facts on command. The standard metaphor was the teacher as the pitcher, pouring knowledge into the student, the vessel. While this format may have been functional at some time (if somewhat limited), it became instantly obsolete with the advent of the personal computer and the Internet. No teacher could possibly hope to match an Internet-equipped student's ability to access information. The mind of the brightest professor pales in comparison to even a rudimentary computer in this function. The job description for educators was no longer "font of information." And yet schools struggled to find uses for their new computer technology while maintaining the obsolete format for instruction. With this historic reliance on methods of delivery like the lecture process, the instructional technology available to students in most schools and colleges is essentially a thousand years old.

The potential of the learning paradigm shift that accompanied the dawning of the Age of Information made schools in their traditional format obsolete. Now, not only are schools one of a number of community entities involved in the education process, the advent of Internet technologies has stripped them of their role as the primary dispensers of information and learning. As Lewis Perelman stated, "If 'school' means a building-bound organization, there are only two qualities of school in the world today – the hopelessly backward and the merely obsolete" (1992).

The Endless Shuffle

The 20th century in education featured an endless array of school reform efforts. Starting in earnest even before the turn of the century, the ranks of school reformers included several presidents of Harvard University, countless college and university professors, and a dismal parade of "education" governors and presidents. The unique feature that all of the reform efforts had in common was that they all represented variations on the same basic paradigm with its uniform set of assumptions. Like any sound bureaucracy, education has gone through the motions of reform while carefully maintaining the original format. The basic process of reform in any static institution is to attempt to improve performance by enacting the old, standard procedures with greater intensity, for a longer period of time. The absolute last resort was to examine the essential nature of the operational paradigm and determine if it remained valid.

Educators have become expert in this process. Schools have experimented with longer days, longer school years, longer and shorter instructional periods, and an endless array of accountability testing programs. The one thing they dare not touch is the basic format of students coming to a central location to be spoon fed information by teachers. This is the fatal flaw in school reform. Any educational reform program that is based on the premise that school is a place, and teachers are the dispensers of knowledge, is doomed to failure. Reforms that insist on fine-tuning an obsolete system, built on an antiquated paradigm, are essentially exercises in "suboptumization," a term economist Kenneth Boulding defined as "trying to do well what should not be done at all" (1964). *No Child Left Behind,* and virtually all reform programs based on the old school paradigm, are efforts to re-arrange the deck chairs on the Titanic!

The obvious question at this point is, "so what?" We have been hearing calls for reform for over a century and American education keeps chugging right along with barely a hint of recognition. During the last two decades of the 20th century, education was deluged with reports with alarming titles like *A Nation At Risk*, and yet little if any substantive change is evident. So the question remains, what is so different now? What makes this call for action any more urgent than those of the previous century? The difference is in wild cards.

The Wild Card Event

A wild card is defined as an event that has a very low probability of happening, but a very high impact when it does. Wild card events can be the result of technological innovations such as the invention of the airplane, the development of the computer, or the splitting of the atom. They can also be caused by natural events such as earthquakes, meteorite strikes, or plagues.

Early in the 20th century America experienced a dramatic, natural wild card event that had profound impact and serves as a sobering warning of potential future dangers. On the morning of March 11th, 1918, a young private reported to sick call at the Army Hospital at Fort Riley, Kansas. He complained of a fever, sore throat, and headache. By noon that day, the hospital had more than one hundred soldiers with the same symptoms. At the end of the week they had five hundred. It was the beginning of the worst epidemic in U.S. history.

Due to advances in medicine and microbiology, researchers, by 1918, had developed vaccines for many bacterial diseases including smallpox, anthrax, rabies, diphtheria, and meningitis. Doctors knew that this latest illness was spread through the air, but the limited microscopes of the time were unable to see tiny viruses. The disease was incorrectly identified as bacterial. Based on this faulty information, ineffective vaccines were developed and administered. Conditions became so dire that then U.S. Surgeon General Vaughan concluded, "If the epidemic continues its mathematical rate of acceleration, civilization could easily disappear from the face of the earth within a few weeks" (1918). Americans responded by hiding in-doors, isolating themselves from their friends and neighbors. Public health agencies distributed masks, forbid spitting on the streets, and closed schools.

For no apparent reason, the epidemic abruptly began to vanish as suddenly as it had appeared. By November of 1918, the number of fatalities had rapidly decreased. Modern researchers speculate that the epidemic simply ran out of fuel. There were no more people who were susceptible and could be infected, thus ending a wild card event that killed more than six hundred thousand Americans and twenty-two million people worldwide. The number of Americans who died from the 1918 Influenza was greater than all of the American combat fatalities of the 20th century. It is sobering to realize that this pandemic rapidly spread across the world in the era before the age of modern air travel. A similar wild card event, either natural or manmade, could immediately shut down America's schools once again. Eighty-three years later, at the dawn of the 21st century the United States witnessed a manmade wild card event that changed two paradigms instantly. On September 10th, 2001, one of the authors of this book was in Riyadh, Saudi Arabia presenting a workshop to the Saudi Ministry of Education. The topic was wild card events and paradigm shifts. The next day, teams of Islamic extremists carried out a wild card event that changed two paradigms within a matter of hours.

Various forms of terrorism, used as political tools, have been in evidence throughout history. However the 20th century advent of aircraft and cruise-ship hijacking, with the ensuing worldwide media coverage, created a new paradigm for this form of political expression. During the latter half of the century, the process became almost institutionalized. Armed terrorists would take over a ship or plane and threaten to harm the passengers and crew unless their demands were met. The demands usually consisted of the freeing of political prisoners, a substantial payment of funds, or safe passage for the hijackers to a sympathetic destination. In some cases the demands were a combination of all three conditions. The underlying assumption of the paradigm was the belief that if the conditions were met, the hostages would not be harmed. September 11th changed all of that.

The paradigm for hijacking shifted when it became apparent that the terrorists on the four hijacked planes had every intention of harming not only the passengers, but themselves as well. All of the rules of hijacking and the assumptions used in dealing with this type of situation suddenly shifted. Terrorist claims that the cooperation of the passengers and crew would insure their safety, proved to be false. The terrorists had created a new paradigm. As is the case in all true paradigm shifts, everyone went back to zero. All participants had to start over with a new set of assumptions and rules of operation.

One of the remarkable features of the events of September 11th was the rapidity with which passengers shifted the paradigm from victims of terror. Aided by the use of cellular technology, the passengers of United Airlines Flight 93 were able to recognize that the old paradigm for hijacking victims was no longer in effect. Cooperating with the terrorists would not guarantee their safety; they would be harmed anyway. Responding immediately, the passengers on United 93 shifted the paradigm for highjack victims, fought back, and substantially altered the outcome of this horrific event. The wild card events of September 11th, which had a very remote probability of occurrence, had a dramatic and lasting impact on the paradigms for air travel and terrorism.

While it is true that wild card events are unexpected due to the remote possibility of their occurrence, it is also true that those who are not paying attention to the warning signs around them are more easily and more often caught off guard. America experienced a rash of school violence toward the end of the 20th century. Armed individuals wounded or killed students, at schools, in almost every state in the union. The initial shock and dismay following these events resulted in some parents removing their students from school, but the state of alarm did not seem to last. Educators and legislators responded with an array of laws and regulations, which ranged from creating safety zones around schools to, in one instance, permanently expelling a student who had accidentally left a butter knife in the bed of his pickup truck after helping his family move. To date, many districts still ignore the tradition of schoolyard bullying that has been identified as the root cause of many school violence episodes.

Fortunately, America has so far avoided a paradigm shift in terrorist activity that purposefully targets schools for acts of mass violence. The Middle East has long dealt with acts of terror that have centered on the general population, including school children, and authorities in Singapore recently arrested 31 suspected Islamic militants who were targeting an American school for such an attack. With similar good fortune America has, so far, been spared the deadly effects of viral epidemics like SARS that have devastated other parts of the world.

The sad reality is that all it would only take one major act of violence against an American school, or the possibility of a widespread deadly epidemic, for the paradigm for schooling to shift immediately! Home schooling would no longer be only an attractive option for some. Anyone who had any concern for the welfare of their children would immediately keep them at home. And it would work! We currently have all of the technology needed to provide a quality education to all students in the comfort and safety of their own homes.

While we know that the odds of catastrophic occurrences in America are low, we also realize that the events as far ranging as September 11th, 1918, or SARS were totally unexpected and caught whole nations by surprise. Whether it is a fish trying to discover water or an educator trying to understand the needs of the new millennium, it is a certainty that the more informed people are, the fewer surprises they experience. As Louis Pasteur indicated, chance favors the prepared mind. As educators we can afford nothing less!

Ending NASA's Monopoly

Nearly a decade ago, Dr. Peter Diamandis offered a $10 million X-prize as a reward to the first private firm to build a reusable manned space vehicle that could fly to the suborbital altitude of 62 miles and then repeat the mission. Aircraft designer Burt Ratan of Scaled Composites, Mojave, California, is closing in on that reward.

Rutan has recently unveiled his fully built launch and recovery system called the White Knight and SpaceShipOne. The system's operation is similar to the procedure utilized by NASA and the Air Force in the 1940s and 1950s. The White Knight launch system will carry SpaceShipOne to an altitude of 50,000 feet and then launch it into a steep climb. The ship is equipped with manual stick-and-rudder controls for subsonic flight, electronic controls for supersonic flight, and cold-gas thrusters for space travel.

To date, the White Knight launch system has been successfully tested to an altitude of 9,000 feet and the SpaceShipOne has performed well in ground-based testing.

For nearly a decade, the X-prize has gone unclaimed, but if Burt Rutan and his team have their way, it will not remain unclaimed much longer.

Source: Jamie Studd, Final Approach, Model Airplane News, August 2003.

Chapter Four

The Fifty-Year Slide

> For schools, the second half of the 20th century
> provided a wild and bumpy descent into
> incompetence.

For schools, the second half of the 20th century provided a wild and bumpy descent into incompetence. This decline was tied directly to the dissolution of the school's partner in values, the family, and to a general break-up of all traditional institutions in the United States during this period. In retrospect, the degree of change that schools experienced from 1950 until the year 2000 may have been even more dramatic than that which occurred in the first half of the 20th century.

Nominating a culprit for the major paradigm shift in the family, and correspondingly in schools, seems easier than identifying which of the many possible catalysts was instrumental in undercutting these two bedrock institutions. Revolutions taking place in communication and transportation, originating at the turn of the century, seemed to become magnified in the

1950-2000 period. The power of the changes, the shift in paradigms, was not immediately evident in schools.

For example, in great-grandmother's time, there were major technological advances that "telegraphed" a new existence for us all. The automobile, the airplane, the telephone, radio, and later the television were all-important and dramatic events that would alter the way people would behave in the future. At first, these changes had little or no form, but as the advances were refined, the power of each change was magnified and the impact on behavior became more directional.

In the beginning, the impact of the radio was severely limited. Farm families sat around this new tool in the 1920s on cold winter evenings listening to adventure plays and occasional news events. There was access, but it was quite limited by the type of programming and the availability of channels. Participation was passive. By the 1950s, in contrast, there was considerably more access, including visual representations (TV) of what had previously been simple intellectual constructs. By the year 2000, the various applications of media had grown such that each person on earth had, potentially, total access to a multiplicity of viewing points. Cheap worldwide cellular phones, instant satellite-delivered television, hand-held global positioning instruments (GPS), palm pilots, Internet connections – the access points were endless. With each new vantage point came new understandings and, yes, choices.

In great-grandmother's time most American families (90 percent) lived on a farm, and family records will indicate that most marriage partners came from nearby families. These extended networks of cousins, uncles, and sisters and brothers revolved around the nuclear family and encased children in social and normative ties. Somewhere in the middle of the 20th century, the new communication and transportation options were beginning to challenge the 19th century conception of what that family meant. In one brief decade, for example, the leading television show, Ozzie and Harriet (1950s), was replaced by the new and intriguing show Peyton Place (1960s). The daring print media of the 1960s, Playboy Magazine, gave way in the 1980s to X-rated cable pornography. By the early 21st century, the conception of families with like-sex partners was firmly imbedded in the media.

Older Americans would rush to tell you that all of this isn't so new and that they had glimpses of these things in their day. The authors would argue, however, that while they may have had a vision of these things, most persons still acted within the structures and conceptions of the traditional family. Only in mother's time, the 1970s and beyond, did these communication and transportation options begin to radically alter behaviors.

It is interesting to quantify the decline of the nuclear family in the United States by reviewing mobility rates (one in five Americans move each year) and statistics such as the rise of divorces and the length of marriages. When graphed, these data show a rapid acceleration (the so-called S-curve) and climb during the second half of the 20th century. More difficult to see, however, is the impact of such changes on families with children in America. The pattern of child rearing and parenting has undergone a revolution in the past fifty years, and it is the emerging pattern that has dashed any hope of schools remaining a stable institution in a sea of social change. The family is the school's client, and as the family goes, so goes the school. The separation of the family from the school during the past fifty years has destabilized the institution in many ways.

One hundred years ago, in great-grandmother's time, people lived on farms in rural areas. Parents had large families because children represented helping hands at harvest time and perhaps a little social security in old age. Children during this time were under the direct supervision of two parents, mom and dad, and additionally the eyes of relatives, neighbors, church and school authorities. They walked to school, though the snow of course, and there wasn't much opportunity for Mark Twainish mischief. Serious problems were dealt with directly by the parents without interference from non-family members or the government.

Fast forward to the 1950s and we see significant changes in both the family and in child rearing practices. The families had left the farms and were located in the suburbs. Both parents were beginning to work from economic necessity. While that nemesis, the television, was present, it was primarily entertaining kids with not-too-violent cartoons during the "kid's hour." Children's mobility was limited to bicycles or an occasional scooter. During this period, most children stayed in the neighborhood and went to neighborhood schools. The interaction of families, still 60 percent nuclear, was determined by likeness (social, religious, racial). A sense of community was present to "control" children's behaviors at home, school, and in the community.

Neighborhood schools, steady church attendance, and institutions like little league baseball, scouting, and social organizations supported the nuclear family, two parents raising biological offspring in a tightly-knit community. By the year 2000, in contrast, only 6 percent of American families were nuclear with only one parent working. The children no longer attended a neighborhood school. Church attendance was way down. The average child in America was watching television six hours a day. Many families were non-biological. The communication and transportation paradigm shift had occurred.

It was in mother's era, the 1970s, that these drastic changes began to accelerate, as it is during this time that the early paradigm shifts were finding application. The car, a source of universal mobility in America, promoted a kind of non-permanence and instability in the workforce. People moved away from familiar family locations and supportive family members. Even children, upon turning sixteen, could get a license and become part of this roving band of Americans.

The airplane, a turn-of-the-century (19th) miracle, had, by 1956, become a part of the public transportation scene. In 1956, the first commercial jet aircraft whisked persons from place to place. At first, the public dressed up for these special occasions. By 2000, the novelty gone, armies of travelers in tank-tops and flip-flops would routinely board aircraft for exotic destinations (Australia anyone?). No longer dependent upon Hollywood for a glimpse of the good life, we could now go there, anywhere, today, and experience places for ourselves.

The idea of mother, and later father, just staying home and giving up twenty prime years to haul kids to little league and piano lessons or to instill lifetime values by planning family outings was losing appeal quickly. The media, in the second half of the 20th century, seduced women and men to live more fully. The Kinsey Report (1953), in particular, was widely read and discussed. An entire generation of Americans was convinced that they were living dull lives, not getting their fair share of sexual fulfillment.

These things are quite easy to see and reconstruct from Census data and various government studies. Not so easy to examine was the emergence during this same period of what might be called "surrogate parenting." The pattern of parents driving or walking their child to the neighborhood school each day quickly transformed into kids climbing on school buses to be driven twenty miles to a school so that court-ordered quotas could be attained. Work patterns forced parents to drop off their kids at daycare before school and necessitated fleets of jitney buses to pick up small children and transport them to predetermined spots after school. Less fortunate children, many not poor, were destined to return to an empty home (latchkey kids) for hours without adult supervision until the parent arrived with the fast food dinner.

And those parents? Of those still trying to carry out the old family scene, most were stretched to the breaking point by their work obligations and the demands of their new lives. They trafficked between their jobs and the maintenance of the "home," perhaps overseeing the life of an elderly parent whose life was prolonged by modern medicines, before finally attending to the needs of these children – children with needs and wants unparalleled in modern times. Increasingly, during the last twenty years, these same parents also chased a social life; one they felt was deserved after working so hard. Tennis lessons, yoga, massage, leisure travel, and perhaps an afternoon delight on the side to round out their fair share of the good life in America.

From the perspective of the school, these are the "good" parents, the ones who, no matter how busy, will still respond to an inquiry about their child or come to the school for a conference about their child's performance. But there are multitudes of "new" parents out there much too busy with their lives to care about their offspring. Between the fractured families (for example a 60 percent divorce rate in Florida), the blended families (yours, mine, and ours), the girlfriend/boyfriend families, the step-in-this-step-in-that families, one-parent families, and the like-sex-we've-got-rights-too families, there hasn't been much contact with schools.

Ask anyone who attended school even forty years ago how many kids came from such family structures and they'll tell you they knew of one or two. Today, the volume of kids from non-conventional, and simply screwed-up, families is staggering. The family is the school client, and without the family, the school is adrift. Today, a good teacher-parent conference is two biological parents who show up, airing their gripes as they proceed to divorce court. Hey, at least they showed up!

In the 1960s, educators and government officials worked to assist a small number of students (perhaps 10 percent) from what was euphemistically called "disadvantaged homes." These students typically had only one parent living with them, were poor, often suffered neglect or abuse because of the social relations of the remaining parent, and came to school without social or survival skills. Academic readiness and motivation in such students was non-existent. Today, there are so many students in school with this profile that our schools are buried in surrogate parenting activities. The decline of the American family has dragged schools into roles such as feeding, dispensing medicine, providing psychological services, accommodating endless special needs, babysitting, and caring for wayward children.

This is the setting for understanding the educational institutions of the 21st century. As practicing educators for most of the second half of the 20th century, your authors have watched schools slide into this abyss. Schools and families are out of contact. There really isn't a clientele for schools any more, and certainly there is no constituency to appeal to for assistance when the schools need a friend. The lines of communication about school services or school reform have been disconnected. The paradigm shift has run its course, and the schools stand alone.

Slippery Slopes

Those Americans over age fifty can tell you about the "good ol' days" in public education. Those days were last seen in the 1950s in an age of *Father Knows Best* and *Ozzie and Harriet*. The television show *Happy Days* (1960s) recreation of those times is fairly accurate in portraying school as it was. It was all so simple then. Schools were populated by "likes" (socio-economics, race, religion, educational attainment, and values) who agreed on what schools should be. For the majority, schools were a preparation for college, a part of the American dream following World War II. And, even though only about 20 percent of all high school graduates even attended college, we were a nation of wanna-be professors. Higher education was an unchallenged destination for all children.

Allegiance to the universal goal of becoming college-educated was strengthened by the new and upwardly mobile middle class. These parents returned from World War II ready to make any sacrifice to give their kids a shot at the good life. Not only was education, in Eisenhower's words, the "cheap defense of a nation," but schooling was widely perceived to be the route to the upper echelons of a professional existence. People believed this in the 1950s – as they do in the 21st century.

In contrast to today, the economy allowed for father to work and mother to be home. It was expected that families eat meals together. There were family outings. Children were made to do homework. The three channels on TV were generally too fuzzy to watch for very long. In a word, it was calm.

There is a myth that education in these days was superior to education today, but in reality schools were simply mindless. Children attended and studied the stuff we all know (names, dates, oddities of subject matter), but many students dropped out of school, and very few actually went to college and completed the experience. Even today, in the early years of the 21st century, only about 10 percent of all living Americans are college graduates. Ten percent! But this is changing rapidly as an over-population of colleges and universities results in lower standards to compete for students. The completion rate for high school (about 72 percent) is at an all-time high as we write this book.

Of course, a high school diploma had far greater value fifty years ago. It was the entry-level education for the world of work. Still, the dream of becoming rich and famous followed the road to college, and for that reason, parents in the 1950s tolerated a curriculum that served almost no one.

The parents whose children were least served by the school, the poor and uneducated parents, were silent and powerless; they were ignorant of the variables that bring school success. Parents today, of course, don't even have time to think of such things.

In reality, nobody but a few college professors spent much time contemplating the role of schooling in America. Schools, like churches and taxes, were just something that everyone experienced. Parents in the 1950s wanted nothing more than peace: a family, a job, a home, and church on Sunday. Schools, though already quite dysfunctional, were what kids did until they grew up.

Some unknown soul has observed that if Rip Van Winkle had gone to sleep in the 1890s and woke up in the 1950s he would have felt most comfortable in a school. Despite the fact that the nation had ceased to be a country of farmers, had urbanized, undergone an industrial revolution, witnessed miracle breakthroughs in communication and transportation, and emerged as the world leader after two global wars, schools were pretty much unchanged. The buildings where children attended school in 1950 looked just like those they attended in 1890. The curriculum they mastered was the same old "going to Harvard" stuff that the Committee of Ten prescribed in 1892. But, instead of 200,000 kids in high school, as there were in 1890, there were now millions. The schooling experienced had grown into a fifteen thousand hour marathon of seat time to become a high school graduate. The curriculum was now a series of lock-step boxes, with some add-ons, to be mastered for a credit.

Teachers in the 1950s were an odd combination of women (some married), returning war veterans re-entering the workforce, and persons between jobs. Since the curriculum was rationalized by content rather than child development, the preparation and qualification for becoming a teacher was simply "knowing a subject." Not many pedagogical (teaching) skills were required in this period, largely because students were still under the control of their parents and troublemakers could be expelled or failed without much introspection. School practices were simply not questioned.

All of this tranquility and simplicity began to dissipate in the late 1950s, although it took school leaders nearly twenty years to recognize the slippage in the foundation of public education. Two events, a Supreme Court decision and a technological achievement, got the ball rolling. A new age of education was emerging in America, and the greatest of all American institutions would now begin a fifty-year slide into chaos and discord.

Slipping

The initial event that signaled a new era for American education was the U.S. Supreme Court decision in the case of Brown versus Topeka (1954). This decision overturned the long-standing Plessey versus Ferguson (1896) ruling that had guaranteed "separate but equal" rights for all citizens. The Brown case was focused on school children and their access to educational opportunity; reflecting a widely-held belief that it was schooling that held the key to success in adulthood.

Linda Brown, an eight-year-old living in Topeka, Kansas, had to walk past a school two blocks from her home to board a bus which took her to a dilapidated older school for colored children. Her parents sued the school district, challenging the "separate but equal" concept. The case ended up in the United States Supreme Court where Kansas and twenty other states were given new parameters for their services to students.

The Brown decision was passed by the Court without any regard to how the decision should be implemented or enforced. Quickly, lawsuits followed, challenging the equity of dual school systems for white and colored children. The lower courts, and then again the Supreme Court, ruled that the races would have to be "integrated" as soon as social tolerance would allow.

Initial efforts to test the segregated systems in the South at the secondary level led to violence and confusion in places such as Little Rock and Greenville. Not only were communities adamant about keeping their traditional high schools "traditional," but the secondary level also painfully displayed the disparity of unequal school systems. When placed in previously all-white schools, adolescent Negro students were often unsuccessful academically, despite their having been chosen for integration because of their academic performance in their previous school.

The dilemma of how to combine these two unlike populations of children, black and white, without sacrificing academic quality, was a puzzle for school leaders and civil rights activists. The final solution, after unsuccessfully blunting heads on secondary school doors for several years, was the "little children" approach. According to this premise, if the integration of black and white children were to begin in the primary grades, the unequalness of the two populations would be minimized. Starting with the first grade, school districts would integrate by adding a grade each year, a twelve-year process to full integration.

The history of this activity is well-documented in the press, but is not well-known to persons under thirty-five years old today; those born after 1970 have lived in a time when efforts to integrate have diminished. Beginning around 1960, very formal efforts were made to integrate public schools in the South (former slave states) where most minority children lived. Efforts were restricted to the elementary grades and revolved around two key issues: school readiness and basic skill mastery.

The Federal government, under then President Kennedy, became the aggressive sponsor of desegregation activities using a combination of court decisions (court orders) and Justice department sanctions against school districts and their officials. Little by little, in district after district in the South only, schools became populated by both white and black children. And, like a bathtub filling up, the ratio of children in the southeastern section of the United States who attended an integrated school rose slowly.

Two logistical problems dogged these efforts for nearly fifteen years, from 1960-1975. First, was the simple problem of how to put children who lived in separate neighborhoods into the same school. The entire history of American education prior to this time was one of local control of schools with neighborhood schools housing children of like backgrounds. The solution, both volatile and expensive, was a massive bussing effort. In many southern districts, continuing today, children rode twenty miles one-way in a yellow school bus to attain access to previously segregated schools. In some of the court-orders, judges gerrymandered attendance lines to create "pie-shapes," "paired districts," and layered districts to make the numbers "work." Now, all southern public school children were little Linda Browns.

The chaos resulting from these efforts is difficult to convey, even though your authors were active participants in these processes. In some districts, as many as 80 percent of all students rode school buses before and after school. In many districts, a single child would change schools five or six times in twelve years, often with totally reconstituted school populations, in order to meet the court-ordered quotas. Parental allegiance to public schools in general declined markedly during this period, and non-traditional private schools gained a foothold in many communities. But the public schools were integrated, and justice was done in the South. Even today, such bussing can consume as much as 10 percent of a district's total budget, which might otherwise have been used to hire a teacher, build a school, or purchase supplies.

A bigger problem for those overseeing the logistics of school integration, and one still with us today, was how to combine two grossly unequal school districts while still maintaining academic integrity. The range of achievement in many of the newly integrated schools was as much as one year for each year attended: a four-year gap in fourth grade, a six-year gap by sixth grade. Imagine the plight of a classroom teacher at the sixth grade level trying to instruct students with a reading range of six years! As it worked out, a concept called "strategic leniency" was employed informally and quietly in most schools, allowing minority children and poor white children to perform less well but still be awarded passing grades. This practice reached its zenith in the late 1980s when many districts created "special benchmarks" to qualify minorities for entrance into gifted programs. As distasteful as this practice was to teachers from previously all-white schools, the dual standard was employed quietly and efficiently throughout the southern schools.

Knowing that such a strategy would be indefensible in the long run, the Federal government under President Johnson pushed through the Elementary and Secondary Education Act (1965), which provided a host of programs to help minority students succeed in newly integrated schools. The public knew of some of these programs due to television (for example, Sesame Street and Electric Company) and programs in the community (Head Start). In schools, a continuum of compensating programs was created, including Title I and Project Follow Through, to help minority and poor children succeed. This distinction of helping one group of children, sometimes at the expense of others, and the reallocation of resources to accomplish these ends, would begin a fifty-year struggle among various constituencies for their "piece of the pie."

In a nutshell, the integration of public schools following Brown broke all of the previous rules for public schools. There would be no more "like" populations in school, no more neighborhood schools, no more local community or parental control at school. There would be dangerous rides on rickety yellow school buses, unequal academic standards (and later quotas), and the disproportionate allocation of scarce resources to special populations. All of these changes mandated by the courts under the "law of the land."

A second unsettling event occurred in 1957, the launch of Sputnik 1 by the Soviet Union. This first-ever satellite, a 183-pound object, orbited earth beaming down a message of friendship to the populations below. America was stunned. Infuriated!

At the conclusion of World War II, the Four Powers (United States, Britain, France, Russia) met to determine the fate of the many territories previously occupied by the Axis Powers (Germany, Italy, and Japan). Transcripts of these meetings revealed that the leaders of the U.S., Britain, and France, excluded the Russian leader (Joseph Stalin) during most social events. Stalin was perceived to be a crude man, a leader of a nation of farmers and peasants, and certainly not the social equal to the other Allied representatives. Thus it was nearly mind-boggling when a dozen years after these post-war meetings the Russians displayed the technological capacity to boost a satellite into outer space and use this instrument to beam down propaganda on others.

The immediate effect of Sputnik was to reactivate those traditionalists who viewed education as the technical act of conveying subject matter. Demonstrating a knee-jerk response, something that would characterize American education for the next fifty years, the United States Congress swung into action. Without study or serious debate, Congress concluded that it had to be our inferior schools that had placed America into the number two position behind the Russians. Leaders in Congress quickly identified science as the single most important subject in school and created the National Science Foundation. This body of scientists and mathematicians were charged with returning the United States to first place in the world in education. A budget significantly larger than that of the entire U.S. Department of Education was allocated for this work. New standards and a new curriculum would be created. This embarrassment would be overcome. Schools would need better buildings, new libraries, new textbooks, and certainly better prepared classroom teachers.

The notion that the Russians might have simply captured better German scientists at the conclusion of World War II did not figure into this reaction from the United States Congress. The importance of Sputnik, in hindsight, was to tie education and schooling directly to our nation's standing in the world. Such a focus continues to this day, with constant referrals to "world class" schools and comparative testing among the nations. Our schools were critical to defense, to nation building, and to catching the Russians.

The positive result of establishing the National Science Foundation was to begin a new era of professionalism in education, and to initiate the renewal of various curriculum subject matter that had remained untended since World War II. Some very serious intellectual activity took place in the 1960s that still pays dividends in school today. The major downside of that sequence of events and activities was to thrust the Federal government into the critical position of leading schools when it was not constitutionally permissible. The public education systems were the sole responsibility of the states, and from this time on the federal role would be unreliable and always political.

When Sputnik is viewed in tandem with the Brown case, one is struck by how much these two events polarized educational efforts in the second half of the 20th century. Brown was about individual rights and human differences. It was, ultimately, the primary funding source for the poor and sometimes incapable students of our nation. Brown suggested a general and citizenship orientation to schooling. Sputnik, by contrast, was about intellectual superiority and academic standards. Educators who followed this path did not even consider the plight of the poor or the effect of environment on education. They simply wanted excellence at any cost. Equity and excellence became the twin peaks of the education world.

And so by the last years of the 1960s, American education was a two-headed dragon with a schizophrenic agenda. For a decade longer schools would pursue these two agendas simultaneously, in a frenzy of spending for a multitude of purposes. But as the Vietnam War wound down, and inflation struck, education would harden into two opposing camps; the intense political battle for control would begin in earnest.

Sliding

If American schools began to lose their footing in the second half of the 20th century, the fifteen years following Sputnik witnessed the uncontrolled disintegration of those things established in the first half of the century. The careful accretion of the subject matter, laboriously added by caring scholars, was scattered to the winds. Conversely, the years of patient construction of a student-focused curriculum was challenged by the complexity of our new society. By the early 1970s, American education was in complete disarray.

The efforts of the National Science Foundation and private universities to restructure math and science instruction in schools resulted in new curricula very different from the old 1890s fare. It was determined that the difference between what was known and what was taught in schools was enormous. To close this gap, academicians stepped in to "help the educators." It was assumed by these college types, as it still is today, that "knowers" were also "teachers." Nobel laureates headed several exclusive groups of advisors to help the teachers turn knowledge into curriculum.

While the academics were solely focused on showing teachers about scholarship, the teachers were equally interested in showing the professors about learning. Infused throughout most teacher training institutions in the United States is a concept attributed to John Dewey, which holds that learning results from student activity more than teacher activity. Because a teacher talks, it doesn't follow that a student learns. At the public school level, the diversity and extreme differences in student backgrounds would mean that any teaching strategy would be as important as the substance of the subject matter.

The blending of these two unlike worlds, the "Greek" universities and the "Roman" public schools, resulted in a kind of thoughtful uncertainty as the various projects to restructure the curriculum unfolded. Jerome Bruner, a Harvard professor and spokesperson for the academics observed:

> Producing curriculum turned out to be not quite as we academics thought! Something a bit strained would happen when one caused to work together a most gifted and experienced teacher and an equally gifted and experienced scientist, historian, or scholar. There was much to be learned by both sides and the process was slow and decisions had to be made about the level at which one wanted to pitch the effort – the College-bound, the "average," or the "slum kid?"

Some of the new curricula in the 1960s and 1970s were, of course, mindless applications of advanced knowledge carried down to the lower schools. AAAS science, for example, used 180 plastic bags to organize the daily lessons on the premise that teachers would not understand, remember, or use the curriculum. But most of the efforts in this period were more conceptual and intuitive in nature. There was, early on, an awareness that the learners had to be activated and that there had to be a relationship of some sort between the curriculum and real human affairs. These were the keys to motivation for learning and utilization of knowledge.

This long stretch between the pure academic research knowledge in math and science and the desire to have American children understand and use this knowledge was the key to revamping a totally obsolete public school curriculum. Unfortunately, in order to fix the American public school curriculum, it first had to be clearly defined. No one body in the United States is responsible for that task, and for most of the projects of the post-Sputnik era the target was never in the sights.

Perhaps no example of "fuzzy" thinking about curriculum reform can top the work of mathematicians during this period. Reacting to the oncoming binomial era of the computer age, the math community sought to instruct students in "bases" under the label "new math." We live in a base 10 society, but all computer operations are simply 0,1. When classroom teachers took the new math and began to teach children to count (0,1,10,11) in base 2, parents scratched their heads.

Reading was also a target; teachers and the "helper professors" developed at least seven different ways to help children understand. Most parents had learned to read using basal texts and memorizing vocabulary. In the new programs, children were taught "decoding skills" (phonics) and to use their own backgrounds and knowledge to increase motivation (whole language). The various methods, sequencing, materials, and evaluation were confusing and contradictory. Again, parents were badly confused.

In quick succession, as money became available, various subject areas were commissioned to reform their areas of study. The totality of these efforts, running roughly from 1958-1968, is referred to in educational literature as the "alphabet projects" era; most of the curriculum titles were so esoteric that only initials (AAAS, BSCS, PSSC, FLES) were used as reference.

The Alternative Education Period

The implementation of the various alphabet curriculums was made difficult because of American teachers' basic lack of understanding about the purpose of schooling. Under the old "two paths" model, everything and nothing seemed to be appropriate. Even more difficult for the implementation of these reforms, however, was the very unfortunate fate of the reforms of the 1960s to be caught up in the emerging diversity enlightenment of the same decade. The reader will remember that in the years following Vietnam, the social fabric of the nation was torn apart by racism, feminism, and the youth movement. In schools, an uneasy balance was struck between the seemingly incompatible demands for equity and excellence.

These were disturbing times in education, and for many, the reforms of math and science curricula raised ugly questions about relevance in public school learning. The reforms of math and science were quickly followed by social studies, language arts, and the related arts (physical education, art, music). Outside forces were demanding a piece of the pie (black studies, women's studies) and an end to what was later called the "dead white man's curriculum." Early jostling began in competition for available reform dollars and quickly became court issues to determine where the ultimate authority resided. Christmas in schools was out, black history month was in!

Adding to the general chaos of the period was an influential book by Charles Silberman entitled *Crisis in the Classroom* (1970). Silberman, a former editor of Fortune Magazine, borrowed heavily from a similar study by Joseph Mayer Rice (1892) and declared that everything was out of control in the public schools. Originally appearing as a serial feature in Playboy Magazine under the title "Murder in the Classroom," Silberman's book was nonetheless given sacrosanct status in the national press. His blow-by-blow accounts of educational screw-ups led to the generic observation that it was all "mindless" in our schools. This same technique of discrediting education would be used again in the 1980s by conservatives in the report *A Nation At Risk* (The Commission on Excellence, 1983), which began with the humble observation that "if an enemy of the United States wanted to destroy our nation, they would create our public schools."

The transitioning of the American public school curriculum from an obsolete and irrelevant pile of facts to the more trendy but indefensible set of "new stuff" accelerated and proliferated until the end of the 1970s. In one high school, where one of your authors served as a consultant, eleven hundred students could select from nearly three hundred separate courses while matriculating toward graduation. All graduation standards fell away during this period, as everyone was allowed "under the tent." Consequently, the price of this new individualized education rose dramatically. At the same time, achievement on the standardized tests (Scholastic Aptitude Test, California Test of Basic Skills, Iowa Test of Basic Skills) declined. Oddly, a severe secondary school population decline occurred naturally from post-World War II times.

A final factor during this period of experimentation with the curriculum, and one that haunts public schools today, was the Mario Fantini notion of a "public school of choice." Fantini, the dean of education at the University of Massachusetts and a social activist, believed that all persons had the right to a relevant and personalized curriculum experience. The implication of this idea was that there could be no common core of learning in an America with so many diverse groups. He advocated, therefore, that schools offer as many curriculums as necessary to serve the diversity of an emerging America.

Schools, now quite punch drunk from a decade of directionless change, followed with the concept of "schools of choice." Berkeley, California, was an early leader, delivering thirty different kinds of schools in a relatively small district. The schools of choice would later become the magnet schools of the 1980s and the charter schools of the 1990s, and would even provide the rationale for the "home schooling" movement of the 21st century.

Diversity issues and simple inflation converged to "kick the skids" out from under the public schools of America. The very foundation of public schools, to provide a common experience and preparation for living in a participatory democracy, was challenged. If all groups, or all individuals, were able to experience the "school of their choice," who could rationalize this institution? More important, who would continue to pay for it? This question was certainly discussed in many state legislatures in the 1980s. The onset of heavy inflation in the 1970s, 12 percent per year or better for eight straight years, resulted in the inability of anyone to support the alternative school movement further. The grand experiment, the attempt to personalize public school learning, crashed to the ground. It has never recovered.

It should be noted that the termination of a free and open-ended educational system, fed by unchecked federal spending, was also assisted by the lack of any true concept of an "alternative" to traditional education. Certainly, there were a wide variety of instructional patterns displayed during the 1970s in free schools, alternative schools, and new private (white flight) church schools. Most of these passing fancies had a theme, but few could conceptualize any essence of education beyond mastering subject matter. Only the most existential programs like the Summerhill model in England (or the Sudbury schools in the United States today) were able to put the same old stuff behind a more important organizer like "freedom."

A wave of exciting books, such as Ivan Illich's *Deschooling Society*, coaxed educators to throw off the old irrelevant curriculum and repressive system of education and "to create new learning communities" without schools. When stripped to the bare essentials, however, most of these writers were talking about the process of education as a form of knowledge acquisition. And, unfortunately for Illich, these writings were twenty-five years in advance of the Internet. At the time, nothing was more efficient as a means of transmitting knowledge from one generation to the next than the time-tested public school. Confusion, indecisiveness, and uncertainly prevailed in the educational establishment as the 1980s approached.

An Age of Accountability

The end of the 1970s witnessed a dramatic change in the form and purpose of public schools in America. The "good times" came to a rapid halt due to the same dogged inflation that drove President Jimmy Carter from office. People's income and state financial resources were badly eroded for nearly a decade. If one looked at schools as only a business or government function, the cost was spiraling upward, despite a declining enrollment and falling achievement scores. The promises of the romantic critics of education, the reformers, were largely unfulfilled. In fact, what remained in 1980 was a sad residue of experimental programs and a school curriculum without boundaries or even priorities.

The election of President Ronald Reagan, former movie star and Governor of California, ushered in a new era of conservative government at the national level. The fifty states, all suffering from a bad economy, followed the national trend from fiscal necessity. Most local school boards were also in a state of disarray; strung out with insufficient property taxes and no real vision of what education should be. Along with a conservative president and state legislature came a new kind of school board member, unhappy with high school taxes and dissatisfied with schools.

One of the most important changes during this era was the shift of the financial burden for schools from the local to the state level. Because the word "education" does not appear in the United States Constitution, support of schooling is a state's right and responsibility. However, since the first schools originated in local communities (a 1647 Massachusetts law required the school when fifty families lived in proximity) the tradition of schooling in America was by "local control." Budget problems changed all of that in the 1970s, and the percent of local effort fell from 60 percent to 30 percent; in the same period, the states picked up the 60 percent effort and the federal government filled in the final 10 percent. And, with state control of educational funding, state politics entered our schools.

The Reagan agenda at the national level was conservative in every way. He demonstrated the "new way" early by calling for general "deregulation" in all walks of life. When challenged by air traffic controllers, who thought deregulation would be a bad idea at airports, Reagan fired them. In education, he mandated the pullback of federal support for education by 10 percent. While 10 percent of 10 percent may seem minuscule to the reader, in some districts the federal effort represented 50 percent of all resources. The new "government without compassion" was in full swing.

The code word for education in this new era of fiscal conservatism and increased political control of schools was "accountability." The word had a nice ring to it at the local school board meetings and was often used in the same sentence with the phrase "back to the basics." In the 1980s, no one in schools knew exactly what these words meant in an operational sense, but they dominated professional journal themes and conference speeches. As the conservative agenda took hold and picked up steam, an amazing transformation of American education was about to take place. Under the pressure of the political policies and money of the Republican Party, education caved in almost without resistance.

An earlier event in the early 1970s under President Richard Nixon, just before his impeachment and removal from office, could have tipped off an observer to the future pattern of the conservatives in taking over education and our schools. Using the new banner, "accountability," the Nixon administration experimented with privatization in education using "performance contracts" as the vehicle. A private company, the Dorsett Corporation, was allowed to take charge of teaching children to read in a school in Texarkana, Texas. In this widely publicized event, Dorsett was to be paid according to how much achievement the corporation could document in working with poor Hispanic children using a very primitive form of stimulus-response psychology (the token economy).

In this program, children who achieved were given credits (like green stamps) that could be cashed in for consumer items like toys, calculators, and even televisions. The experiment with performance contracting to private businesses ended when the Dorsett Corporation was caught teaching the test to the children. Nixon, preoccupied with Watergate, withdrew from the effort to capture the schools.

Accountability was also used to introduce "testing" as the measure of achievement in schools during the Reagan period. Using a business model, schools were expected to demonstrate and document a measurable "bang for the buck," just like those businesses in America who were accountable to their stockholders and constituents. Little was said then, or now, about the fact that each year in America one-half of all new businesses fail. Today, no one speaks of the repeated revelations that American corporations have shamelessly manipulated the stock market and returns for decades. The analogy sounded good to the taxpayers!

The school leaders, superintendents and principals, under the scrutiny of newly elected conservative school boards, marched in lock-step (perhaps even goose-step) in connecting fiscal expenditure to achievement productivity. The old subjects, the 1890 stuff, became the new curriculum. Everything except reading, writing, and math took a back seat in the schools.

For the next twenty-five years, up to the time of this writing, many of the other subjects would not even be taught regularly in some districts as they focused on "scoring" points on standardized achievement tests. Curriculums were skewed and unbalanced for greater curriculum productivity and efficiency.

In the beginning, targeting the curriculum was difficult for businessmen-turned-educators. America had survived for nearly a century with a two-headed school program, focused on both subjects and the student as a person. About the best outcome available at the time was the Scholastic Aptitude Test (SAT) produced by the National Testing Service in Princeton, New Jersey. This test was reported religiously in the newspapers like some kind of ball score as *the* measure of America's schools. Finally, when it was noted that aptitude and achievement were not synonymous, the test lost favor. By some quirk of fate, it was determined that the scores of districts on this test corresponded closely to the socioeconomic level of the community being measured.

There followed in the 1980s an attempt to introduce "international" achievement testing as a measure of excellence in American schools. A conservative press reported time and again how American children were at or near the bottom of the ladder among advanced nations. A book by Biddle and Berliner, *The Manufactured Crisis* (1997), put this mythology to rest among professional educators. The book clearly revealed that the top 10 percent of children in nations like Germany were being compared to the upper 50 percent of American children taking the same test. Head to head, our 10 percent matched anyone's 10 percent. But the public bought the story: "Hey, I read it in the newspaper."

Conservatives in the 1990s would later make up their own education system, including teacher certification (National Board certification), standards-based curriculum (America's Choice), and other parallel entities.

But the big break through for the takeover of American education came when the far right stumbled upon the idea of just making up their state tests. Using the Chief State Officers (elected state commissioners of education) as a vehicle for dissemination and enforcement, state after state passed accountability legislation requiring educational competencies as measures of achievement. This "standardization" was to be measured by locally constructed tests, the new basis for promotion and graduation.

As this agenda was unveiled in state after state, it did not at first seem to threaten the historically rich humanistic curriculum. Early efforts to hold all students accountable to identical standards, no matter how minimal the standards, seemed foolish. Any teacher could tell you that children differ greatly in their backgrounds, abilities, and motivation. In Florida, for example, promotion testing was conducted with vigor from 1980-1985 at Grades 3, 5, 8, and 11. Any child not performing at grade level was retained (failed). State education leaders abandoned this testing hurriedly when nearly one-third of all students in the state were held back. A study showing that the state had never graduated a double-retainee led the state to pull back before the drop out rate became even larger.

Still, it is true that public agencies tend to follow the funding, and control of funding for schools was now squarely in the hands of state legislatures. Basic education, reading and math first, was an established fact of life in America's ninety-five thousand schools by the late 1980s, and the mandated testing programs quickly squeezed the life out of any subject not tested. The public school curriculum was once again unbalanced, skewed, and irrational.

During the final two decades of the 20th century, the conservative pressures on public education took numerous forms; many of which took professional educators by surprise. This was the era during which the Republican Party was using massive funds from PACs (political action committees) to secure large majorities in Congress, the governorships, and state legislatures. It was also a time when the Reagan administration was appointing large numbers of federal judges to the benches of our courts. Additionally, wealthy conservatives like Rupert Murdoch bought up many prominent newspapers and television stations. For the first time, some black politicians joined the Republican Party, and some professional educators professed loyalty to the conservative cause.

It has previously been mentioned that competency testing movements in most states narrowed the curriculum of schools to the study of what was to be tested. There were also serious efforts to redefine what should be taught, such as Mortimer Adler's *Paideia Proposal* (1982) and E.D. Hirsch's *Cultural Literacy: What Every American Needs To Know* (1988). These works were praised in the conservative media as the way schools should go. Finally, there were propaganda efforts, clear and simple, in the various media to convince the public that their schools needed changing. "Walking Tall," the story of a tough inner city Los Angeles principal, and another story about a Chicago principal who overcame the ghetto with "tough-love" were widely disseminated. Most of the success stories, like the "research" on basic skills programs, proved phony upon closer inspection.

In the newspapers during the late 1980s and early 1990s, papers still read as gospel by the public, there were stories of various commissions who issued scathing reports about our schools and their performance: *A Nation At Risk* (1983) blaming schools for our nation's decline, *A Nation Prepared: Teachers for the 21st Century* (1986) blaming teachers, *Turning Points* (1989) calling for families to get involved in fixing schools, *Goals 2000* (1990) targeting broad goals for all schools, SCANS (1992) Department of Labor calling for teaching workplace skills in schools.

Of these many calls to action, none seemed so compelling to the public as the February 1990 report *National Education Goals – Goals 2000*.

Born from the unprecedented meeting between the President of the United States, George Bush, and the fifty governors headed by soon-to-be-President Bill Clinton, this group sought to set target goals for education by the year 2000. The attendance of all fifty governors, and their signatures on the document, seemed to somehow overcome the historic reality of education being a "state's right." *Goals 2000* represented the first-ever national policy on education in America.

In reality, the document was full of "political wind," and unattainable upon delivery. It was quickly relegated to a pile of other such documents by professional educators, but still played well in the media. *Goals 2000* promised that all students would start school ready to learn. It promised a graduation rate of 90 percent by the year 2000. It promised that the United States would be number one in mathematics achievement in the world by 2000. It promised that every adult in America would be literate by the year 2000. It promised drug-free schools by the year 2000. The list goes on, but for the sake of brevity, this bill was hogwash to professional educators who wondered, "What are they thinking about?" The public and the media, however, loved every one of the goals.

Professional educators reacted to the goal that every child would start school ready to learn through the lens of Head Start, Title I, and Sesame Street. These massive and expensive programs, in their thirty-fifth year, had failed to make a dent in the socioeconomic determination of school performance. Silk purses from sows' ears just wasn't going to occur soon. And, as for the 90 percent graduation rate, most educators knew that the best-ever figure of high school completion was around 72 percent and that figure was declining. Being number one in math in the world was, at best, a pipe dream (whatcha smoking boys?). And adult literacy? It stood to reason that if between 30 and 40 percent of the present adult population did not complete school, and only 10 percent of the total population had graduated from college, there would be some major illiteracy. The goals of *Goals 2000* were simply preposterous!

By this time, of course, it didn't matter what the educators were thinking, because they were definitely not involved in reforming the schools. Reform was a political thing, and teachers had already been painted as money-grubbing, union types. Business "elected" legislators who then introduced legislation that was hailed by the media and turned over to re-constituted state departments of education for implementation. Bullying schools and teachers with sanctions, withholding funds, and humiliating low-performing (poor) schools in the press was now standard procedure. The relationship between lawmakers and educators was adversarial and acrimonious. As Governor Jeb Bush of Florida publicly stated in his 2003 inaugural address, "the educators have resisted us and we have defeated them."

Last Exits

As the politicians pursued their educational policies from 1980-2000, spending more and more to do less and less, their system refined itself into obsolescence. Several huge changes in the environment that might have reversed what amounted to a "fatal" flaw in policy were overlooked. The first was the arrival of special education in the late 1970s and the other was the arrival of the Internet in the mid 1990s.

Until around 1910 in America, children were perceived as miniature but incomplete adults. They were characterized as somewhat evil in nature, necessitating the occasional "beating the devil" out of them. The prevailing impression of young people began to change with the first physiological studies of youth and the birth of American psychology in the early 20th century. Soon, physical and psychological (intelligence) differences were noted by educators. Carl Jung's model of psychological types (1921) ushered in the new era of student-centered education in the United States, an education system noting the uniqueness of both children and adults.

The period from 1920-1980 was one of massive research in education, with particular emphasis on the study of human differences. The Stanford-Binet scale defined the wide range of intelligence in school children. Various studies of children (Bessell, Havighurst, Piaget) gave educators models for understanding student development and performance in school. Later, research in areas such as gender difference and multiple intelligences led an entire wing of American educators to actively seek ways to serve all students. Progressive education, born in John Dewey's school at the University of Chicago (1896-1904), dedicated itself to finding teaching procedures to match the many learning styles of the students attending our public schools.

By far, the most dramatic kind of differences among students attending our schools were those in "special education" categories who exhibited what was originally thought to be handicaps for learning. Containing these students in special segregated schools for the deaf, the blind, and the mentally deficient made sense in the early years of the 20th century. But an activist political system allowed parents of such children to petition Congress and demand relief from such apartness. The idea that children with handicaps would encounter more success in school if not isolated from their normal peers gained acceptance at the highest levels of government in the 1970s.

In 1975, the 94th Congress passed a bill known as the Education for All Handicapped Children Act (known as 94-142 in schools) which created federal protection for the rights of all handicapped children attending school between ages three and twenty-one. Based on six principles, the legislation guaranteed that all children who were capable would be "mainstreamed," or placed in regular public school classrooms. The parents of these children were made full partners in the process and their rights were backed by the force of the federal law (due process) and its courts.

Over a fifteen-year period, through good economic times and through the worst of economic times, the public schools of America pressed forward to make the idea of handicapped children in regular classrooms work. New kinds of teachers were prepared to work with some ten different categories of learners. Eventually, these so-called handicapped children comprised 14 percent of all public school students in America, and in some districts consumed up to 40 percent of all operational resources.

By the mid-1980s, the mainstream model was failing because too many children with special needs were being excluded from the regular school classrooms. Once again, the parents of these children took their grievance to the U.S. Congress and once again Congress responded in 1990 with the Individuals With Disabilities Education Act (IDEA- 20 U.S. Code 1412). This new law mandated that "children with disabilities will be educated with children without disabilities and that no separate channels should be supported except under direst circumstances." Known as Inclusion in Schools, the act effectively placed all special students in regular rooms, in many cases with classroom teachers who had no training in working with the handicapped. Special Education teachers were spread around to help these regular teachers to the best of their ability.

While this experiment continues as this book is being written, Inclusion demonstrates the degree to which American educators had accepted individual differences in children. Today, some thirty-five labels are used to describe these differences in schools including disadvantaged, emotionally handicapped, deaf, non-English speaking, and so forth. What a far cry from only one century earlier when all children were perceived as the same!

Yet, from 1980 onward, like an ostrich with its head in the sand (or perhaps elsewhere), the conservative agenda for schools pressed to make all students perform alike. Competency testing compared and contrasted all students by the same criteria, the score on the standardized test. It was as if one hundred years of forward progress in knowing children and working with them through acts of teaching had just evaporated.

The desire of some to see public education as a kind of race or contest, and the inability of the traditionalist to dovetail standards with human differences, represented the first massive breakdown of the public system. Carried to its logical conclusion, the system would evolve into a dog-eat-dog, "save the best and shoot the rest" mentality. This is close to where schools are as this book is being written. The beat goes on!

The final exit point for this now "sick" system was the appearance of the Internet in schools in the mid-1990s. Had public schools recognized this event for the paradigm shift that it was, they still might have been able to pull back from standards-based education and reform themselves for another century of useful service. However, it didn't turn out that way.

Computers have been with us for nearly a half-century or more in America. Originally quite large due to vacuum tubes, the smaller computers with micro-technologies date from the 1960s. Public purchase of microcomputers, or personal computers (PCs), first occurred in the mid-1980s. The Internet, today so much of our existence, was first available to the public in May, 1995.

When the public was first able to buy personal computers in stores, schools were already using computers for operations such as scheduling and payroll. Therefore, the early interest of schools in personal computers was primarily for public relations and image. Suddenly, the outside world was very excited about these little computers, and other walks of life (government and business) were using them for an increasing number of tasks. Any school

116

in the late 1980s without a few of these little computers around would be unfashionable.

Schools bought their first PCs without giving much thought to their function. The Texas Instrument model with "speech" was trendy. The Commodores seemed sturdy and business-like. The Apples had student-friendly software. So, at first, schools collected these machines and placed them in highly visible places in the school like the office and library. Before long, in the late 1980s, most schools could report on surveys that they did indeed have computers and some were even being used for student instruction.

The real problem with the early personal computer was the absence of good software. The programmers were still creating software with commands, and many schools used their computers in the beginning to teach student how to "program." By the late 1980s, new edubusinesses had moved into this niche market and were beginning to produce software for learning. The focus of most of this early software was basic skill mastery. Over a five-year period, the Apple II.e. established itself as the "standard" workhorse for schools, and federal and state funds were used to purchase enough of these tools to form "labs." For a couple of years, such labs were indistinguishable from regular classrooms except for the computers; students took their seats and worked through the prescribed software.

Toward the end of this phase of computers in schools, educators were able to wire up computer networks (local area networks, LANS, and wide area networks, WANS) so that students could even communicate with a class across the hall or in another building. Major dollars were invested in this 1985-1995 period, but most of the applications were limited to skill-drill and content coverage. Not much actual computing took place in the classroom.

Suddenly, upon the scene came the most amazing breakthrough learning has ever known, the Internet. Actually, this network, or networks, had been around since the time of the Vietnam War under the military name AARPNET. By the 1980s, a special National Science Foundation version (NSFNET) was in use. Finally, business interests convinced Congress to make the tool available to commercial interests and the Internet was born.

Schools were puzzled, and still are, by the Internet. Here was an information retrieval device so superior to anything previously known or imagined that it defied comparison. It was a savant, capable of holding, retrieving, and processing unlimited amounts of knowledge – able to give and get knowledge in an instant. The Internet instantly made textbooks, libraries, and even teachers obsolete as a primary source of knowledge. School children could use the device to learn anything! Traditional schooling was challenged to understand and absorb this new wonder, this massive paradigm shift, without disrupting America's largest single institution. There were no instructions from the government and no real help from the universities. Every school was on its own to accommodate the changes coming from the presence of the Internet.

It would be a pleasure for the authors to report that, in the first eight years following the release of the Internet to the public, schools adjusted and began a complete redesign of learning. Unfortunately, such a report cannot be made now, nor will it be made soon. Instead, the fact is very few of America's thirteen thousand school districts have used the Internet in any serious way to improve classroom instruction. Approximately one-half of all classroom teachers report that they use the Internet (for email and information searches), but not at school. Schools are simply stymied by this force of electronic learning, and many actively discourage use of the Internet in classrooms.

The five-year horizon for Internet use is both exciting and quite scary for schools. The technological gadgets schools are so fond of purchasing with public monies will keep coming and continue to be great fun. Because storage of information will become external within five years (not stored on your computer but in cyberspace), the size and form of computers will be more varied. Voice recognition and miniature and wearable computers will mean the cell phone, a TV, or even a broach can serve as a vehicle for receiving and sending information. Heads-up technologies mean that our eyeglasses or even the windows in our home can serve as computer screens.

Also to come, soon, are additional Internets. The monopoly of the English-speaking world ended in 2003 when more non-English-speaking persons were on the "net" than English-speaking persons. Around 2010, more Chinese will be using the Internet than all other groups combined. Political uses of the Internet are a distinct possibility as we look ahead, and schools will have to deal with this challenge to academic freedom in a manner more effective than they have dealt with the issue of pornography.

In all probability, learners will leave the public schools to be serviced by private enterprises that will fully understand the allegiances of the consumers. The entertaining Internet games of the 1990s will become the format for the highly interactive and personalized form of learning provided by the tireless and unlimited purveyor of man's knowledge bases. Acquiring knowledge will give way to an emphasis on knowledge utilization. Whether schools can understand this distinction and gear up for some new kind of delivery system is highly questionable. If, as Robert Gagne has observed, "learning is limited by what the learner perceives," we will be a nation of haves and have nots based not on wealth, but on the ability to adapt to the changing environment.

In the largest sense, this technological paradigm shift is not about teachers' jobs, or the ninety-five thousand school buildings, or the textbook publishers' future. Organized knowledge has been the basis of cultural and social transmission and renewal since the beginning of recorded history. If the "new order," in the form of learning under the guidance of advanced technologies, has no common denominator, we will quickly become a nation of non-aligned individuals. Our allegiance will be commanded by those knowing enough to capture the media that shapes our perceptions.

Schools, as we know them, could only survive this paradigm shift if they reallocated resources to construct new infrastructures. Investment in equipment, software, training, maintenance, and telecommunications would have to be directed toward a future in which the learner, not the teacher, is the key player. We would have to cease constructing the monument buildings, leave the tens of thousands of school buses behind, build a close and different relationship with families, rethink teacher certification, establish non-standard evaluation measures, and redefine what we mean by "curriculum." These things have not happened in any form in the past eight years, and they will not happen. The paradigm shift brought about by the Internet has still not been recognized by school leadership.

Free Fall

So, what happens next? A unique school system dedicated to two masters, knowing and growing, has finally been captured by a traditional and conservative coalition of business, religious, and political entities. The century-long experiment, unique in this world of nations, has been largely snuffed out by political pressure, court actions, and, most of all, the shortage of funds. A whole generation of teachers has now completed a decade where testing more for less is the sole mission of schooling. The system has become closed, refining itself into greater and greater obsolescence. The last decade has seen that very system attack its own teachers, starve its students, and completely miss the most important change in teaching and learning in a millennium.

Our public schools are dying! They are dinosaurs from the 19th century, soon to be populated by only the poor and uninformed. They will, for a while, only serve the two-class world envisioned by our nation's conservatives. Little worker bees will be produced to Department of Labor standards to carry out the lesser functions of society, while the privileged will wallow in the rich soup of our technological future. This divide, this separation of peoples, has been a failing recipe for societies since the beginning of time. The "magic" of an inventive America will be vaporized.

And what about the parents who can understand these words and fear for their sons and daughters as they trudge each day to the little red schoolhouse? These parents, we believe, must begin to look out for themselves. As Paul Simon's song *Set Yourself Free* enticed us, we need to "get a new plan Stan." Parents must define a future for their children and act to alter the path that is presently laid out for them by those now driving the education boat. Our next chapter explores what some of those steps might be.

Economic Futures Lab

The Policy Simulation Laboratory at the University of Rhode Island is being used to create artificial environments to test new economic markets. One of twelve facilities of its kind in the United States, the Rhode Island lab employs paid volunteers to enact economic scenarios that can be used to determine future regulations affecting the state's development. The lab was used recently to study proposed lobster fishing license changes.

Rhode Island's current fishing license allows fishermen to set 800 traps. Since some individuals want to set fewer traps and others would like to set more, the state is considering the establishment of "tradable allowances," which would allow lobstermen to trade their right to sell some of their traps. The lab exercises enabled the participants to compare profitability and distribution issues under the proposed alternative trading rules.

The lab has 26 high-tech work stations, 2 group discussion rooms, and a 125-seat presentation hall with advanced audiovisual aids and in-seat voting capabilities. The interactive computer technologies can simulate the environmental, economic, and social impacts of potential policies, giving leaders a clearer picture of how their decisions might impact whole communities. Since it was opened in 2001, the lab has been used in 20 to 30 scenario exercises per year.

Source: University of Rhode Island, Kingston.

Chapter Five

Dark Horses

> The fascinating aspect of this vision for the new
> 21st century learning is that the technology is
> largely in place to do all of these things.

That our present system of education is broken beyond repair is obvious to anyone who closely inspects the rusting machinery of schooling. A more relevant question for inquiry is, "Can our schools be replaced by something else more functional?" Replacing an institution of such proportions and importance is a frightening proposition, much like changing jobs, or getting a divorce, or dealing with death. Things will never be the same once we commit to the substitution. For the authors, thirty-year veterans of the old way, the answer is an affirmative "maybe." We can leave the school, and we can find true education in the 21st century in America, but this change will be a low bet, a dark horse, for sure.

The mechanics of abandoning ninety-five thousand school buildings, possibly textbooks in all subjects, a three million person teaching force, the testing industry, and hundred of thousands of school buses, are fairly clear. American education must begin to push away from this 19th century institution and enter the technological mainstream of the new century. A full menu of possibilities will be presented in this chapter for the reader's consideration. Not so clear, however, are two questions: 1) "What will the new education look like?" and 2) "Who will be responsible for education in the future?" The authors will try, in this chapter, to project some possible and probable futures in these two areas.

Before There Were Schools

In medieval times, education transpired without schools, curriculum, textbooks, or tests. Renaissance scholars learned from an impermanent group of wise persons who came and went, serving as loose guides to information. There were no authoritative sources of knowledge like there are in today's school.

Until just after our Civil War, individuals in America gained knowledge through many available sources including the church, home, schools, mentors, and personal study. Knowledge was not catalogued, scheduled, or graded. It did not exist to divide persons into piles or serve an industrial purpose. Knowledge just existed, and it was consumed by individuals for many reasons. Education was shaped to individual circumstances, not to social expectations.

In America, as we have seen, schools were formed almost immediately for the purpose of teaching the young to read (the Bible) and for general civic literacy. Higher learning at the universities was largely unstructured in the 19th century. Universities and colleges were comprised of a collection of scholars and persons (students) who wanted to learn. There were no actual or even inferred connections between learning and work or position. All of this changed, of course, in the late 19th century when schools and higher education defined the various courses of study and completion requirements. At this moment, schools became social programming mechanisms; schools began serving social ends rather than personal ends.

The power of schools is found in their ability to identify and define what counts in learning. The use of textbooks, standards, and examinations all control learning and, by exclusion, cause other forms of learning to be irrelevant or of questionable worth. One is "educated" by the prescription of the school. As the credentialing agency, a controlling power, the school is able to put itself above the interest of the individual. In the United States, we all submit to such control and direction because of the widely held belief that education is the path to jobs, social status, and wealth. This probably is not true.

Ivan Illich, a visionary writing in the 1970s, saw school as depriving some individuals of an "education," and even perpetuating the existing social order as surely as a fence can divide properties:

> Will people continue to treat learning as a commodity – a commodity that could be more efficiently produced and consumed by greater numbers of people if new institutional arrangements were established? Or shall we set up only those institutional arrangements that protect the autonomy of the learner – his private initiative to decide what he will learn and his inalienable right to learn what he likes rather than what is useful to somebody else? We must choose between more efficient education and a new society in education which ceases to be the task of special agency.

The important point to be made here is that we have arrived, in recent history, at a point where schooling is not synonymous with education

When our schools evolved into social instruments to direct learners (train, not educate them) and define their "education," they did so to serve social purposes. For example, a widely held goal for most public schools is to develop in pupils an allegiance to the principles of democracy. Students don't get to assess democracy for its own merit, and are not educated until they have mastered the identified principles.

As general media expanded in the 20th century, threatening the exclusiveness of the school as the purveyor of knowledge, structures such as syllabi and the textbook were used as vehicles of control. The "curriculum" made the student a dependent of the teacher in the learning process. The fact that teachers were found after 1900 exclusively in schools, gave the impression that schooling and becoming educated were the same thing; this perception has kept education from reforming itself for a century.

Education in a Technological Age

Imagine how you would feel if one day your next door neighbor came home with a new kind of automobile that could fly, didn't need fuel, and had every driving option known to man on it. Imagine the combination of freedom and luxury! Would you still be satisfied with your old gas-guzzler that has to share the crowded highways with others, or would you covet your neighbor's new car wishing you could have the same advantage?

Education in the technology age is a lot like this car story. Most of our children are stuck in an obsolete, immobile institution that has failed for half a century to make a significant adjustment to the changing world we live in. That new machine, not tethered to old investments, is sitting nearby, waiting to be used. Yet, no one in the school world seems to recognize that this single tool, the computer with Internet connection, can take us instantly from the 19th to the 21st century. We all have been in "school" so long we are prison dumb, unable to even imagine something else.

The current institution operates like a ship without a rudder, serving multiple philosophies simultaneously. It is impossibly expensive, and it is inefficient. Worse, the school, as an institution, does not want to change; it cannot change. By contrast, the new machine promises the following:

1) Instead of linear learning, it promises multimedia convergent learning.

2) Instead of instruction, it promises construction and discovery.

3) Instead of teacher-centeredness, it promises student-centeredness.

4) Instead of memorization, it promises exploration and navigation.

5) Instead of place-bound learning, it promises learning anywhere, anytime.

6) Instead of promoting learning as work, it promises learning as natural, fun.

7) Instead of the teacher as transmitter, it promises the teacher as a facilitator.

In a nutshell, this is a new machine that can take us from those crowded and often irrelevant learning places to a higher plane with greater success for all. We should be envious of anyone with such a superior vehicle for becoming educated. All we have to do is say to ourselves, "education is not schooling." We have the tool to provide a superior delivery system for learning and one that is more adaptable in delivering knowledge to students than any teacher. The Internet is the library of all libraries, and the computer is the teacher of all teachers – if only we would consider the possibilities. Let's begin by looking at some of the alternatives to straight "school."

Sorting It All Out

Professional educators, government officials, and even the general public have stuck by schools through thick and thin because, as stated earlier, education and schooling are perceived as one. This connection, this association, has prevented true educational reform in America. In fact, learning and knowing are not the same, just as education and schooling are quite different.

In one construct presented by Nathan Shedroff, learning is made up of five factors: noise, data, information, knowledge, and wisdom. Noise would be random data, received but not ordered. Data would be elements of knowledge, but not in a pattern. Information would be data that is formed into a pattern. Knowledge would be validated data that appears in a pattern. Finally, wisdom would be knowledge that is validated and applied. What constitutes noise, data, information, knowledge, and wisdom, is contextual; it depends upon the conditions for learning.

Learning could be defined as the process of turning information (patterns of data) into knowledge (validated patterns). By such a definition, schools provide a useful function by storing, validating, and transmitting important patterns of data from the old to the young. This role worked especially well in the 19th century when what was known to be important was catalogued and controlled by scholars, schools, and books. But, in the 20th century, media dispersed noise, data, information, and knowledge in such volume, and in such complex forms, that telling the important from the unimportant became a serious problem. For schools, this was the relevance issue, and it lies at the heart of all curriculum.

For knowledge is bounded by what is known – beyond what we know lies what we don't know, and what we don't know, we don't know. The very randomness of not knowing, and, even worse, not knowing we don't know, makes learning difficult. In the old days, one hundred years ago, scholars sorted the data and the information from the existing validated information (knowledge), and applied knowledge (wisdom). But the speed and the volume of technical knowledge (technology), has disrupted this timeworn process. Today, other sources of information, such as the radio, television, travel, and computers, have given us all access to noise, data, information, knowledge, and wisdom. It is no longer particularly exclusive. Further, we have all been presented with the opportunity, or necessity, of judging these sources situationally according to our personal needs. Rock and Roll music may be noise to some and a favorite love song to others. Who, today, has the right or the ability to judge the worth of the various information sources bombarding us?

Two questions confront us today: "What is the best way to learn?" and, "How can we best give value to the information sources?" The old answer to both of these questions was, "trust the school." Today, this is the wrong answer. Even though the school will sort out, organize, and validate the voluminous data for us, there is not an appropriate context for doing so. Do we believe that what was true in the past is the best preparation for the future? Some educators (traditionalists) believe this, but most do not. Our lives and society in the early 21st century are complex and dynamic. The wisdom of the elderly hardly seems applicable to the young. As Margaret Mead put it, teachers looking backward toward the past meet students facing forward toward the present and future.

To be wise today, the educated person must be able to use or apply learning. The act of become wise is no longer a linear process (1, 2, 3, 4), but rather one of convergence. The relevance of knowledge, and the concept of wisdom, is a situational phenomenon. Using new hardware, such as electronic books, micro-computers, palm pilots, and digital telephones, we have left a world where knowledge acquisition and knowledge storage are valuable. We have entered an era of global knowledge exchange and application. Our old knowledge is bounded by what we don't know, and the schooling process is the culprit. What we need to be able to do is "connect" our existing knowledge to the unknown. As we enter the 21st century, our learning structure (the school) is not up to this task. As Alvin Toffler has observed, " the illiterate of 2000 and beyond will not be the individual who cannot read or write, but the one who cannot learn, unlearn, and relearn" (1970).

For centuries our schools have defined education as "knowing," and the schools we possess are virtual monuments to knowledge acquisition. All of the practices of the modern school are about the control of learning and the measurement of knowing. Our little knowledge factories, oddly enough, are nearly void of wisdom; there is little if any connection or application of knowledge to our dynamic and changing world. To speak in the vernacular of our age, the school is a dead portal when it comes to wisdom.

One might ask, "Can't our schools change?" Both authors are experienced educators with over thirty years of practical experience in schools. In order for our schools to even begin to respond to the kind of paradigm shift being outlined in this book, the following would have to occur:

- New avenues for learning and communicating would have to be designed.
- Standardization of the curriculum would have to be de-emphasized.
- Human differences and capabilities would have to be acknowledged.
- New facilities would have to be envisioned and constructed.

- Huge sums of start-up capital for technology would have to be expended.
- Large investments in technological training would have to be allocated.
- A new kind of teacher would have to be recruited and rewarded.
- Teachers and students would have to be networked and allowed freedom.
- Knowledge would have to be valued for its application, not acquisition.

An indication of how difficult any of the above would be to accomplish can be gained by looking at the present facility needs of American education. In a 2003 study of facilities, "Modernizing Our Schools," by the National Education Association, it was estimated that to repair, renovate, and install modern technology in existing school would cost $322 billion. This is approximately ten times what the fifty states are currently spending (or borrowing to spend), and four times the cost of the War in Iraq. School facilities in America have been largely ignored since the inflationary period of the 1980s. Under present circumstances, and the flatness of the American economy, designing and building new age facilities seems highly unlikely.

It is the experience of your authors that these things, redesigning education for the 21st century, won't happen. Indeed, it is impossible that these kinds of changes could happen within the framework of our decentralized educational network. As the old consulting line goes, "resurrection is always more difficult than giving birth." It is really time for America to move on, to find some new options and a new portal for learning in the 21st century.

Unlimited Alternatives

There are numerous, almost unlimited, alternatives to the American public school system at the time of this writing. While it is beyond the scope of this book to try to catalogue these options, we can observe that America has always had options other than the public system. In addition to religious schools, like the Catholic system, there has been a continuous stream of private institutions, alternative schools, free schools, and now home school options. These options all represent a search for a way around the monolithic and mandatory public school.

There has also always been a continuing call for reform in books like this one, some shrill, like John Holt's *How Children Fail* (1964). Observing that schools are a "tell 'em and test 'em" sort of place, Holt called for an exodus from a "jail-like place where students bide their time to get out." Grace Llewellyn's more recent *Teenage Liberation Handbook: How To Quit School and Get a Real Life and Education* (1997) was another call to escape from the "cells and bells." Ivan Illich, previously cited as the author of *Deschooling Society* (1970), advocated the end of school in order to end the "one size fits all" orientation of mass education. Matt Hern, in his the recent book *Deschooling Our Lives* (1997), called for the escape from the corrosive effects of compulsory schooling.

Your authors recognize all of these alternatives education forms, and criticisms of the present school form, as legitimate pleas for change. But as successful products of that very system, we see a better reason for changing. More than repression, bias, and a jail-like environment, the reason we should be leaving the school is to find true education. The institution we presently use to educate our children is sadly obsolete and not competitive with the option of e-learning. All of the other institutions in our society know this and have moved toward a reconstruction of how they communicate, learn, and process knowledge. The school, a place to learn, is dysfunctional in its design, procedures, and results. This is why we must begin to dismantle this institution.

Alternative Portals

During the 20th century, an increasing number of Americans desired a release from both the practices and the institution of the school. The Progressive movement, from 1920-1940, provided many non-conforming school experiences, as did the Alternative school movement of the 1970s. Even today, in the midst of arch-conservative control, magnet schools, charter schools, and home schooling provide choices beyond the mainstream of compulsory public education.

The motivations that drive these groups to " get out" are many. Some seek religious freedoms in school. Some seek relief from the political dimensions of the school curriculum. Some seek to escape persecution or discrimination. Some are reacting to government policies. Many parents feel that basic learning services are lacking in the free public schools of America. Regardless of the motivation, all of these efforts represent hard work to develop an option for children.

The authors would observe that almost all of these attempts to elude the public education system have been based on the notion that a better school could be constructed. Few of these efforts over the past one hundred years have sought to leave the school altogether. We think this condition is simply a result of being too close to schools to be able to see or imagine life without them. This is how we, in the United States, conceptualize education.

An example of this condition can be drawn from the many alternative schools of the 1970s. These institutions were promoted by individuals who felt betrayed or abused by the public system of education. While the alternatives took many forms, almost all tried to reinvent the school – from the format of a school. That is, they still saw education as a building, with a teacher and students, using books to master a curriculum. Most of these 1970s schools failed within a decade for lack of realistic finances, from a defection of the patrons, or from an inability to get accredited by various agencies

While leaving the established school system to construct a parallel and competitive school or school system (private education) was unnatural, expensive, and redundant, the exodus has been continuous. It represents a general migration, by persons in the United States, away from many institutions (churches, industry) that are perceived as unrewarding. While the many forms fail to take hold and grow, there is always a new attempt to change.

The "learning industry" in the United States today is massive. Elementary and secondary schools alone account for the expenditure of $389 billion. Corporate and business education ($65 billion), government education ($42 billion), vocational training ($23 billion), and consumer learning ($21 billion) quantify the scale of this industry. The taxpayer supports much of this industry.

While public schools have not embraced the new learning technologies available to us all, industry, government, and vocational proprietary schools have. It is estimated that about 4 to 5 percent of all training expenditures in business today are via electronic learning mediums. Using these cheaper and more flexible instruments, nearly 30 percent of all corporate training is by computer. Just as our government encourages us to file our federal income taxes electronically, and banks and businesses encourage Internet transactions, the corporate world has discovered the "economy" of training their employees using learning technologies.

From a simple trickle in the early 1990s, the trend of going "high tech" has now begun to "spill over" into education, and soon may have serious influence on the policies and practices of our public schools. A good example of this influence can be drawn from the "home schooling" movement across the United States. Once restricted to a handful of extremists, home schooling today is recognized as legitimate in all fifty states and involves about 1.7 million students each day. While this is a "drop in the bucket" when compared to the other fifty-six million students not home schooled, it is interesting to note that the movement parallels the use of the Internet in the United States. As the Internet, now concluding its eighth year of availability, grows in use, the home school movement follows.

Home school parents have discovered a new industry of distance learning and curriculum software that can duplicate and surpass the public school curriculum. Using these instruments, students at home can learn subject matter, as well as resourcefulness and self- reliance. Such students are allowed a strong degree of independence in learning, engaging the curriculum through multiple avenues utilizing their own style. And, rather than being isolated in their quest for an education, they are able to network with other students on a global scale. Few persons in education, or outside of education, understand the richness of this resource that is at our collective fingertips. In one free site on the Internet, for example, the home schooled student can access the Louvre, the Museum of Modern Art, the National Air and Space Museum, the Field Museum of Natural History, and the National Museum of Science and Technology. Included in this lifetime of learning menu is a guided educational curriculum for anyone wishing to access the site.

As we glide through the middle of the first decade of the new millennium, a number of access points (portals in computer lingo) to this new technological stream of knowledge are emerging. Important for the moment is that home schoolers, students in special magnet schools, charter school students, and private schools using vouchers for tuition, even the parents of students in public schools, can access these resources without leaving the traditional structure of education. Just as the television didn't eliminate the radio as a medium, the Internet is not going to put schools out of business. Not yet, anyway.

What we do need to recognize is that a paradigm shift is underway! Not only are these new learning portals being used by business and private education, but they are also taking serious root in colleges and universities and in most proprietary schools. All around us we see on-line course work, mentoring, tutoring, on-line learning communities, and computer-mediated communication (CMC). As futurist Joel Barker has observed, " you have to look to the fringes of society to understand the change; this is where it takes place first" (1992).

Many of these new hybrids are school-like in their form and function. For example, a student in high school or college can take a biology course through software (CD-ROM), or by distance learning, and these efforts are graded and recorded for credit just like in the traditional school. In Florida, Florida High School is a virtual school attended by some ten thousand students who take some or all of their high school education on-line. Some out-of-state students also attend Florida High. Schools like this one, and the Clonlara School in Ann Arbor, Michigan, are virtual schools that mirror real schools. They operate out of the same "control" parameters as the regular school and, as such, do not fully utilize the power of the Internet. They are technologically driven, but do not use the new technologies as a new way of learning.

What is driving these early changes in private education and proprietary education are the same forces that compelled the U.S. Government, AT&T, the U.S. Army, and other major institutions down the technology street. Business, for example, faces a tight economy, offshore competition via new technologies, an aging work force, demographically driven resource shortages, and new growth industries using technology. Technology is replacing human operators in many jobs, incumbent workers often need mid-career retraining, and the complexity of the changes in our society demand a more personal and prescriptive learning that is aligned with business objects. Said simply, to survive and flourish, they must change!

Because new education forms, private, proprietary, or even public alternatives, must "compete," they are adopting the new technologies as a matter of course. Institutions like the United States Postal Service and the public schools have not been so enthusiastic about changing due to their security as tax-supported public monopolies. Take away the subsidy and watch educational reform take-off.

The authors believe the public schools are already experiencing the beginning of an "end run" past their role as the institution for learning by smaller and more technological services. We liken these changes occurring in the middle of the first decade of the 21st century to those witnessed in the 1990s, just before the U.S. Postal Service was overtaken by Federal Express and United Parcel Service. In a matter of only a few years, the postal monopoly was broken; lucrative trade was peeled away from the postal authorities. As the USPS tried to reform itself by closing offices and cutting back its workforce, it also nearly succumbed to an inappropriate application of technology. Today, over ten years later, the now "kinda technological" postal service is chasing its competitors from a far distance. Spending more to catch up, at taxpayer expense, has not proven a successful strategy.

Our public schools possess a monopoly on "official learning," and have held that position for over a century. From this paradigm, the only learning that counts is school learning, learning that is blessed by the "official" institutions with their credits and degrees. But, if this official learning were not found to be tied to job opportunity, the accumulation of wealth, or positions of status, as suggested in the book *The Great Training Robbery*, then this privileged position stands on tradition alone. And, if it was also found that this great institution was actually interfering with getting an education, then it would be highly vulnerable to defection. And, of course, it is.

Since 1970, in the United States, there has been a creeping intrusion from the business sector to invade schools with the objective of replacing public schools with something else. As early as the Nixon administration (1968-1972), the federal government promoted "performance contracts" to enable business to compete with schools for tax dollars. More recently, the Bush administration has promoted testing and vouchers as a means of discrediting public schools and opening up this $389 billion "market." An additional $261 billion worth of opportunity at the post-secondary and higher education level provides an irresistible target for "takeover." Interestingly, these fairly persistent efforts over a thirty-five year period to "open up" schools have been largely unsuccessful due to the paradigm held by the public: schools are our cherished institution.

If schools are to move from where they are at this point to a new age of learning with a different "vessel," there must be a market created that will draw investors. As the reader will note later in this chapter, that "learning options" market is just around the corner. In the meantime, businesses like Sylvan Learning Systems and Bill Bennett's new K-12 Corporation will begin to skin this carcass. However, the prize of massive financial rewards will not go to those doing the "same ol', same ol'" with technology. Rather, the winners, from a business standpoint, will go to the architects of a new delivery system that bypasses the school.

To the degree that old subjects and school learnings can be put in a new and spiffy format, with bells and whistles like computer games, that preferred format will draw some defectors. But such a migration will be slow and very costly to anyone attempting this route. In contrast, the organization that can provide a medium for personal learning, for a real education unrestricted by the existing monopolistic system structures, the rewards will be staggering. What is needed, of course, is a personal learning machine, and it already exists! This machine is presently a children's toy in the United States.

Such a learning machine would help individuals gain knowledge about things that interest them. It would provide simulations of experiences that can't easily be accessed otherwise. It would provide a medium for social exchanges between persons of like interest. It would provide knowledge paths to guide learners in seeing patterns, and making useful associations and applications. It would encourage exciting learning journeys. Mentors and tutors would be available, night and day, to assist, interpret, or guide the learner. It would have the world's most massive resource base for knowing.

In addition, such a learning machine would keep track of personal learning; never forgetting the learner's previous experiences and achievements. It would assist the learner in forming or joining learning groups. It could proffer topics, links, and applications of information based on knowledge of previous learning experiences. In a nutshell, such an instrument could wipe out the public school experience (that 19th century dinosaur that captures fifty-seven million children everyday) by simply being superior. But, as long as education equals school in the mind of the public, people will remain captured by their perceptions and their paradigms.

Marching in Year Nine

As your authors, both teachers, peck away at their word processors, we are living year nine since the Internet went public (May 1995). We live in a society where most persons now own or have regular access to a computer with Internet connection. Email, or electronic mail, has become a preferred and common form of communication in this short period. Search engines, both of human construction and spider-based (electronic construction), have been modified for convenience and allow anyone easy access to any kind of information. We have all become accustomed to the www. designation in advertising, magazine, and entertainment sources. It is now possible to speak (Naturally Speaking, Natural Voices) to computers, bypassing the keyboard. We have miniaturized the instruments (cell phones with digital and photographic capacity, palm pilots, digital cameras). We have video cams that allow computer users to see each other, and systems like AT&T's Avatar for synchronizing voice with mouth and body movements. We have language translation capacity (Babelfish) that allows communication with persons who do not share our language. We can speak in sign language without knowing how using the Michigan State University site. The fact is that it is not technology that is holding us back from finding an education. The development of new learning portals is a vision thing, an ability to understand and act on the paradigm shift.

It is true that there are some models, in some places, that suggest a transformation to the 21st century might occur if the motivation to realign education could be activated in business and among the taxpayers. At the lowest level, we do presently have the regular old public school curriculum on-line in many places. For example, high school students in Oregon can satisfy their social studies elective for graduation on-line. In Florida, ten thousand students are attending high school on-line.

We also have many schools that are beginning to use non-conventional spaces for learning. The Irvine schools in California (Oak Creek and Canyon View), for example, are building their classrooms for "work teams," student networking, and the use of common technologies such as scanners, printers, and digital cameras. Other schools, following the 1970s Parkway model in Philadelphia, have moved their learning spaces off-campus to abandoned shopping malls and storefronts. Some school districts, like St. Johns County in Florida, are experimenting with issuing laptops to all students, lessening the dependence on paper and pencils, as well as textbooks. Finally, at the university level, distance learning is growing. Western Governors University, aided by a $10 million grant from the U. S. Office of Education, is using virtual technology to train and certify teachers on-line. Phoenix University, a relative newcomer in the external degree market, is now the largest university in the United States by user headcount.

But, while all of these "inside" efforts are noble, they appear to the authors to be a case of "too little too late." Certainly, these hybrids do not reflect the reality of the majority of all schools at any level of education. Most schools do not provide on-line alternatives. Most are not modifying their buildings to reflect the interdependence of the global economy, or leaving the school building to seek other learning places. Most are not providing their students with individual access to outside information channels. Most are not staffing their schools with technology-savvy teachers. In fact, most schools are still holding court in the standard classroom, using aged textbooks, putting small amounts of money into computer laboratories, and fielding change-resistant faculties.

Can you see them? Visit a school and know in advance that nothing has changed. Very few educators are thinking about this at all. And, of those who are concerned, only a handful would follow Stephen Covey's suggestion to "start with the end in mind" (1989). Our educators are very comfortable and secure in their monopoly.

The Pot of Gold

In order to "get there from here," educators will have to envision learning without school buildings. We must experience a paradigm shift that will strip away the blinders that continue to cause us to equate the little red schoolhouse with an education. To quote America's most famous educator, John Dewey, "what the wisest parent wants for his own child, that must be what we want for all children." There is a pot of gold at the end of that rainbow, and we must begin with a vision of that pot before we begin our transition.

Ultimately, the future of education in the United States will require five things in order to construct it: 1) a rationale for learning, 2) a learning place, 3) learning mediums, 4) validation of our learning, and 5) teachers. Let's address each in terms of the future.

The rationale for learning in the present is dominated by the desire to acquire content or knowledge, with an oblique promise that good things will come to those who do so. The new rationale would value knowing, but would require a belief that endless journeys will occur and that knowledge will be defined by individual needs and experiences. Our most human trait is to learn, and our natural motivation to pursue this end must be trusted and unleashed in the 21st century.

Certainly, the trap of equating a school building with learning must fall away as we transition to real education. Today, if an educator hears of a wonderful educational program that is housed in a classroom with a low pupil-teacher ratio, the likely response would be, "Yeah, I'd like to see them try that with thirty kids in the room." What the teacher should be saying is, "We could do that also if we had a lower student-teacher ratio." The knee-jerk response of all American educators is to try to fit the change back into the old school.

With new technologies, the act of learning does not have to be in a school or a classroom. Learning is no longer place-bound, time-bound, or teacher-bound. The fact that we continue to invest billions of tax dollars into 19th century-style monuments that are used about one-third of the time should be a compelling argument for moving on.

Finding new learning mediums or channels is an obvious need for any regular user of the Internet. The phrase "learning communities" will become important since the act of both acquiring and applying knowledge will involve others. A learning community is a group of self-governing people who share values and generate and exchange knowledge for mutual benefit and increased capabilities. Such communities would work within a kind of "learning eco-system" where there is a common infrastructure and common portals for learning.

Using the Internet as the primary resource, future learners might have a group or groups of fellow learners for self-assessment, conferencing, collaboration on projects, and working in virtual laboratories of various kinds. A typical "portfolio" might include such things as my profile, my training, my in-progress work, my networks, my mentors, and my resources. Many of these services would be contractual, with the medium of exchange being either money or reciprocation. There would be, of course, support and maintenance requirements, and a very sharp distinction between the physical and the technological environment for learning.

A fourth prerequisite for the future of education in the United States would be the validation of such learning. Such a validation could be a testing procedure (discussed more fully in a later chapter), but this would be unlikely once our understanding of an education passed beyond knowledge acquisition. More likely, validation would be a kind of competence demonstration depending upon the application of knowing that is chosen by the learner. If, for instance, someone wanted to earn a license to fly an airplane, demonstration of that capacity could occur in many mediums. The person being tested could acquire the information in a traditional classroom, from a mentor, through on-line simulation experiences, or any other reasonable approach.

Finally, something akin to a teacher or guide would have to be available to those engaged in learning. Just as most persons could, theoretically, educate themselves by the experiences of a lifetime, we believe an individual could learn a massive amount with time on the Internet. But the randomness of the knowledge on the Internet, and the impermanence of information on the web (six month automatic expiration in many cases), and the degree of choice on the Internet, all suggest the wisdom of a teacher or mentor. This is as it was from the beginning of time until the late 19th century. Without such a guide, the Internet could easily become a kind of intellectual maze that might confuse and ultimately would disorient the learner.

So, the end that we envision is one of freedom and mobility for the learner, seeking a true education from a sea of rich resources, and accessing that learning from whatever portal seems most comfortable to the learner. Such a learner would be aided by teacher-mentors and learning communities composed of others who share common values and would voluntarily share resources for mutual benefit. The knowledge acquired in the learning process would not be quantified or weighted, but rather would be assessed in terms of its application value. Each individual would have to judge, alone, what knowledge was most important in this short lifetime.

The completion of this circle requires only two things: breaking the fiscal monopoly of the schools, and the creation of a servicing mechanism by free enterprise sources. This transition could be gentle or cataclysmic, but the transition itself seems to the authors to be inevitable. The odds that any one of these "dark horses" will take the winners circle is remote, but they are far superior to the odds that today's schools will reform themselves. The paradigm shift in education has already occurred, and needs only to be recognized by those whose lives are to be affected by this change.

Portals and Potholes

A revolution is underway in American education, and the public and private schools don't even know it. On the inside, most children in school are attending a place similar to the one that their parents and even their grandparents attended. The daily routine is one of pre-cooked lessons, intellectual fast food from the textbooks, and quick-score testing at the end of the week. Their learning tools consist of paper and pencils, and backpacks full of stuff. On the outside, learning is being defined in terms of electronic media (e-learning). Quietly, and without public funding, one-half million sites (search of Google) leading to learning portals have sprung up. Yes! One-half million sites. It is as though our educators are living in a cave.

Corporations have moved decisively toward this new world. Many companies have developed their own "universities": Motorola University, Disney University, Dell University, Microsoft University; the list goes on and on. Driven primarily by the fear of being left behind, businesses have recognized this revolutionary instrument for what it is: a savant, a superior medium. Schools, by contrast, have not even seriously studied Internet-assisted learning. As a monopoly with no serious competitors, schools have found comfort in becoming even more narrow and traditional.

The many new learning portals, growing rapidly as various forms of e-commerce, have exotic names like BigChalk, Click2learn, CyberU, Ilearn, and Mind's Edge. Most of these portals (access points) are being created to service industrial training needs. Rushing forward to claim territory on the electronic frontier, many are ill-conceived. Like so many of the early Internet businesses (dot.com) some of these companies will experience a short lifespan, and therefore are as yet unreliable for learners. We are, as they say, in a "shake down" period of this movement.

The authors see these new portals as one of two kinds, traditional and innovative. The traditional portals have not yet distinguished between e-reading and e-learning. An example of the traditional sort is Lightspan, a portal aimed at schools with the promise of instructing more effectively in reading, language arts, and mathematics through "an engaging interactive curriculum." An example of a traditional site at the university level is free-ed.net, which offers a bachelors and a masters degree using complete courses and tutorials in 120 academic and vocational disciplines. All of this is possible, says free-ed.net without books to buy or hidden fees to pay.

Perhaps the traditional portal receiving the most attention, as this book is written, is the for-profit on-line school, K12, pitched by former U.S. Secretary of Education (and later drug Czar) William Bennett. The K12 organization seeks to offer a complete primary and secondary education, including every core subject, through the home computer. Using a $10 million loan from former junk bond king Michael Miliken (a convicted felon), Bennett has used his influence to get national, state, and local support for the idea.

Bennett's initial target audience would be the 1.7 million home schooled students to whom he wishes to sell diagnostic tests, lesson plans, and materials for about $5,000 per child. Already succeeding in several states, Bennett received $5 million from the Florida legislature to try the K12 curriculum on about one thousand students. Bigger plans for virtual charter schools are on the horizon for the company.

While the authors can quietly admire the shaking and moving this man is doing using old Reagan contacts, his allegiance to what he calls "old school academic achievement" reveals a special kind of ignorance about the potential of electronic learning portals. Bennett's statement that he would like to be for the next generation what the Encyclopedia Britannica was for his generation speaks volumes about his lack of understanding of what the Internet might accomplish for education. He would place "world-class education" at the fingertips of all children, says Bennett, reaching back to his 1982 copy of the *Paideia Proposal*. He claims he would deliver "good content." To this, the authors would shout, " same ol', same ol'!"

The paradigm shift that is upon us in education is not about "good content." It is not about learning more math, or language arts, or science, or history. We have plenty of that in our schools already. The shift in paradigm is about distributive learning environments (Kearsley, 1985) that would provide each individual student with a unique educational experience. It is about removing the classroom barriers that have frustrated teachers forever: the differences in intelligence, personality, prior knowledge, flexibility, and style of learning. It is about accessibility, flexibility, and affordability. It is about new portals that can provide access to learning from multiple sources, aggregating, hosting, and distributing knowledge. Traditional portals, that only provide learners with an electronic book, are merely potholes in the road to a new form of educating.

The hallmarks of the new learning portals, and the electronic delivery and service to learners, will be a sensory-appealing, personalized, and relevant learning experience. Through special and tailored portals, customized learning will be available to all who desire it at a relatively low cost. With each new user, the cost will decline on a per unit basis.

While such flexible and adaptable services are largely unknown to those persons in schools, they are quite common in the world of business. Businesses think nothing of contracting for a service they need that others can produce more cheaply. In the beginning, education portals for the public will be supplemental to schooling, but will quickly become a replacement for the schooling experience once their power has been demonstrated. The authors envision these information/learning services as a pay-option much like your cable television. You can receive basic services, or you can pay for additional options to your heart's content. Below, we provide a preview of what might currently be taken off the Internet, in most cases without any charge. A detailed site listing is provided for the reader in Appendix A:

Basic Four-Window Portal For Individuals
Traditional Education and Training
Information Resources
Self-Assessment and Development
Entertainment and Leisure

Window 1 – Education and Training
Formal education course work from virtual sources
Training for licenses (Driver's license, Real Estate License)
GED and other certifications
Computer tutorials such as Tax Prep
Language acquisition
Conferences on-line
Virtual classrooms
Adult learning

Window 2 – Information Sources
News rooms
World newspapers
On-line journals
Knowledge banks (libraries/museums)
Consulting services / advisors

Music libraries

World of movies

Virtual bookstores

For hire searches

Databases

Window 3 – Self-Assessment and Development

Physical fitness training and nutrition

Intelligence testing

Personality and learning style assessments

Talent discovery and development

Window 4 – Entertainment and Leisure

Virtual learning centers

Virtual vacations

Mood enhancers

Travel on the web

Virtual sports and games

Let's suppose you are using the portal above. A servicing agency would assess your needs and offer a series of relevant sites for your entire family. Nearly all of the following are free on the Internet or available for a low cost to the subscriber. These selections are not projected portal sites; they exist today and can be accessed by the reader immediately. There are as many sites and as many kind of portals as we can imagine. Again, most are free of charge.

What will not be free, in the near future, is the service aspect of the new educational learning. Anyone could, of course, build their own portal or their own networks, but the authors believe that something like an "electronic teacher" will be needed to guide us through the massive choices facing the user. Once again, such service oriented e-companies are already doing business in corporate America. Syberworks, for example, is a company that has been around since 1995 helping organizations with web-based training. Among their services, typical for e-learning, are promoting web conferencing, customizing courseware, encouraging interactive communication among persons with common interests, delivering personal services, and hosting the e-learning portal.

For the authors, it seems feasible that such a service could be delivered to any learner in America, of any age, at a fraction of the cost of the old school model ($7000 per pupil). There would be no costly overhead (buildings, administration, buses, support staff, textbooks, or even teachers). More important, every learner could experience the very best of the best in terms of resources and development activities. All that would be needed are functioning (monitored and managed) portals and savvy guides for learning. And, just as there are "spider" search engines, it would seem feasible that once the learner clients were profiled (known in terms of wants and needs), they could be "catered to" in ways never before experienced.

On the horizon (five years) is the capability of new computers to deliver such learning in a form compatible with the learning style of the student. Using ATI (aptitude by treatment interaction) technology, it would be possible for the learning machine or computer to "read" the learner's preferences and deliver the messages sought in a preferred format; variables might include field independence vs. dependence, focal attention, band width, degree of cognitive flexibility, verbalizing vs. visualizing, color preference, and more. Said more simply, we are soon going to have computers that will note the student's learning habits, based on patterns of millions of learners, and adjust the delivery to the optimal condition for that individual. Just as each of us has a different telephone number, every learner in the new way of educating will have a special menu and a tailored or individualized presentation.

The fascinating aspect of this "vision" for the 21st century education is that the technology is largely in place already. A parent could choose if his or her offspring would be a college graduate, speak a foreign language, develop a talent in fine art, virtually visit the highest culture on earth, and have international learning pals! The parent would simply contract for the service. Heads up display screens (your living room window) and voice recognition technology have your child, or yourself, sitting at home and interacting with the world-at-large. This can happen. This will happen.

Ultimately, the limitations on the development of such a "learning machine" in education are found in both vision and money. The vision, the paradigm shift if you wish, is here, now, to be recognized. The money, the billions and billions stored in school buildings and busses and teacher salaries, is also available; it just has to be unlocked. Given the scale of the learning enterprise in America, the "gold rush" can't be far ahead. First, however, comes the task of uncoupling America from the school buildings, buildings that now absorb the massive resources of our last great monopoly.

Learning Through Virtual Reality

Virtual reality (VR) is a computer-generated 3-dimensional experience in which the user can feel immersed in and interact with another environment in real time. While VR represents a nearly limitless array of future possibilities for learning, it is presently being used effectively in the fields of engineering, medicine, and military technology.

Computers have long been used by engineers as computer assisted design (CAD) tools in the 2-dimensional environments. The development of 3-CAD and virtual reality programs are the natural progression of this technology. Using VR technology, General Motor's engineers claim they can review and modify three designs in the time it used to take to consider one, and discover potential problems before they are turned into expensive physical prototypes.

In the field of medicine, VR currently permits surgeons to test procedures and hone their skills with no harm to patients. Future developments include plans to build an entire virtual human that responds accurately to disease, injury, and medication. Using the virtual human, researchers will be able to study how the various organs individually, and in concert, will respond to medication, procedures, and injury.

The military is also interested in virtual human technology, contracting with scientists at the Oak Ridge National Laboratory to build a virtual human platform the armed services can use to test the effects of a series of non-lethal weapons.

Source: John Briggs, The Futurist, May/June 2002.

Chapter Six

Time to Put Up

> The key issue that has stymied so many efforts is
> the confusion between the concepts of reforming
> education and fixing schools.

Here we go again, a book critical of the field of education! What next? Up to this point, many of the issues we have discussed have been mentioned by concerned individuals for at least a century. Teachers, students, parents, administrators, professors, and politicians have all sounded alarms concerning the state of American education. Today the media is alive with reports of the most current efforts to "leave no child behind."

While there has been an abundance of criticism and alarm concerning the schooling crisis, prior to this book there has been a noticeable shortage of practical solutions. The issue that has stymied so many past efforts at reform is confusion between the concepts of education and schooling.

Most often when we think about the prospect of restructuring education, we begin with an image of how to fix schools. Despite the overwhelming evidence that the traditional school paradigm is broken beyond repair, the initial reaction is to start tinkering with the familiar system. Schools are bureaucratic dinosaurs, so wrapped up in the trappings of their operation that they long ago lost sight of their real purpose: to educate.

In this chapter, we will separate the concept of education from the limits of schooling and discuss many of the elements needed by America to truly educate its populace. We will outline an appropriate role for federal involvement in education, discuss the advantage of replacing politics in education with learning, outline a support system appropriate for the 21st century, establish a new organizational structure to replace outdated grade levels, develop an effective evaluation system for students, teachers, and learning organizations, overhaul the antiquated agrarian calendar, and describe the types of learning opportunities that this new paradigm may offer.

The Paradigm of Purpose

The first paradigm that must be shifted is the role and responsibility of government, at the highest level, for the education of its citizenry. Interest and concern for citizens' education has been evident in America from the time of the Pilgrims. Twenty-two years after the landing at Plymouth Rock, a 1642 Massachusetts law directed: "…certain chosen men of each town to ascertain from time to time, if parents and masters were attending to their educational duties; if the children were being trained in learning and labor and other employments … profitable to the state; and if children were being taught to read and understand the principles of religion and the capital laws of the country and empowered them to impose fines on those who refuse to render such accounts to them when required" (Cubberly, 1920). As Elwood Cubberly noted, this was the first time in the history of the English speaking world that a legislative body passed a law requiring that children be taught to read (1909).

This recognition of the importance of education to the welfare of the state was again expressed in the prefix of the Ordinance of 1787, which the Congress of Confederation enacted for the organization of the Northwest Territory. They stated: "Religion, morality, and knowledge being necessary to good government and the happiness of mankind, schools, and the means of education shall forever be encouraged." While the ordinance applied only to states carved out of the Northwest Territory, it strongly implied that education was a governmental responsibility.

This sense of urgency continued into the early days of the republic as evidenced by the words of Thomas Jefferson in a 1787 letter to James Madison, "Above all things I hope the education of the common people will be attended to; convinced that on this good sense we may rely with the most security for the preservation of a due sense of liberty" (Cubberly, 1920). After his retirement from the presidency, Jefferson wrote in a 1816 letter to Colonel Yancy: "If a nation expects to be ignorant and free in a state of civilization it expects what never was and never will be.... There is no safe deposit (for the foundations of government) but with the people themselves; nor can they be safe with them without information" (Cubberly).

This awareness of the critical value of an educated citizenry continued into the next century, evidenced by the words of Thaddeus Steven's 1835 address to the Pennsylvania House of Representatives pleading for continued tax support for public schools.

If an elective republic is to endure for any great length of time, every elector must have sufficient information, not only to accumulate wealth, and take care of his pecuniary concerns, but to direct wisely the legislatures, the ambassadors, and the executive of the nation –

for some part of all these things, some agency in approving or disapproving of them, falls to every freeman. If then, the permanency of our government depends upon such knowledge, it is the duty of government to see that the means of information be diffused to every citizen. This is a significant answer to those who deem education a private and not a public duty – who argue that they are willing to educate their own children, but not their neighbor's children.

What we see to this point is the purpose for education evolving from one of colonial-vintage morality to one of civic literacy. This evolutionary process continued into the mid-1800s with the arrival of various groups of non-Anglo-Saxon immigrants. Beginning in the 1840s and continuing through the turn of the century, waves of Irish Catholics, German Catholics, Jews, Italians, and other assorted groups from Eastern Europe began immigrating to the United States. Their arrival prompted concern among the Anglo-Saxon majority about the ability and willingness of these new citizens to assimilate and socialize into American culture. Business and educational leaders began to realize that schools could serve as the nation's agency of socialization. Cubberly wrote that it was part of the responsibility of the schools to "amalgamate these people as part of our American race" (1909). Cubberly's reference to the American "race" clearly meant WASPS, but in the mid 19th century another ethnic group was becoming a part of the educational process. African-Americans, who prior to 1863 had not been considered at all in the nation's educational enterprise, were now being included.

As America entered and progressed through the 20th century, the roles of education developed as the nation grew and evolved. With the advent of industrial growth, America's school system developed a curious format in which it served all children with the previously described college preparation curriculum, administered in a factory-like setting.

A Constitutional Oversight

In spite of the nation's historical recognition or the critical importance of an educated electorate for the survival of the democracy, and an adequately trained workforce for the welfare of industry, America is unique among modern industrial countries in that its Constitution does not even mention education. The Tenth Amendment to the United States Constitution indicates: "The powers not delegated to the United States by the Constitution, nor prohibited to it by the States, are reserved to the States respectively or to the people." Due to the fact that the Constitution makes no specific reference to education, it has been assumed that it is the responsibility of the individual states. As a result, the United States had no national educational goals and while there were sporadic efforts to articulate a national policy for education, such as the work of the National Education Association's 1935 Educational Policies Commission, the first real attempt to establish unified goals came when the president and all fifty governors signed off on the previously mentioned America 2000 document.

The exercise of the states' responsibility to educate their citizens, and the individualized approaches they have taken to this obligation, has resulted in a variety of formulas for funding and implementation. These fifty strategies are alike only in their failure to provide an equitable, effective, quality education to all American youth.

The differences in spending allocations from district to district within the same state, not to mention from one part of the country to another, is staggering. Among the nation's districts with fifteen thousand students, some claim to educate students for as little as $3,538 per year (Nebo, Utah), while others spend $12,105 (Newark City, New Jersey) on the same enterprise (Table 93, U.S. Dept. of Education). This difference in expenditures between states ($8,567 per student) is little better when examined within the same state. While the difference between districts' per-pupil expenditures in a single state are typically less than $2,000, in some cases they may be considerably more. For example, the difference in per-pupil spending between Newark City District, New Jersey, and Tom's River Regional District, New Jersey, is $3,892 per student! The states' district averages when compared on a state-to-state basis are no more encouraging. During the most current years recorded by the U.S. Department of Education, the difference between states, in terms of average district expenditures per student, ranged from $10,145 for the State of New Jersey, to $4,210 for the State of Utah – a difference of $5,935 per student (Table 169, U.S. Dept. of Education). This gross inequality in educational spending is, to a degree, the result of the system that has been traditionally used to fund public schools.

Where Does the Money Come From?

The universal assumption about the process of taxation is that taxes represent funding that is raised for the common interest or the public good. The power to impose taxes is inherent in the sovereign rights of an independent nation. In the United States, both the state and federal governments have been vested with the power to tax. While there is a seemingly endless variety of taxes imposed by both the state and federal government, it is the property tax that has been the mainstay of public school funding. The term "property tax" may refer to tangible personal, intangible personal, or real property. The tax on real property has been historically the main source of revenue for public schools. Property taxes also have a long history of unpopularity. As early as 1776, Adam Smith discussed the inequality inherent in property taxation in *An Inquiry into the Nature and Causes of the Wealth of Nations,* "A land tax … necessarily becomes unequal in process of time according to the unequal degrees of improvement or neglect in the cultivation of the different parts of the country. In England the valuation according to which the different countries and parishes were assessed to the land-tax by the 4th William and Mary was very unequal, even at its first establishment." Nearly a century later the sentiment expressed concerning property tax was no more flattering. "No other tax in our public finance system bears down so harshly on low-income households, or is so capriciously related to the flow of cash into the household. When compared to the preferential treatment accorded outlays for shelter under both the income and sales tax, the property tax stands out clearly as an anti-housing levy. Moreover as the tax increases steadily, it is viewed by a growing number of families as a threat to homeownership…. The property tax is more painful to pay than the 'pay as you go' income and sales taxes" (Shannon, 1973).

Lack of popularity aside, the major problem with the reliance on property taxes to fund public education is the disparity in funding resources that this system provides. Areas with lower property values and a lack of business and industry to aid in the contribution equation have fewer dollars to spend on education. Affluent areas, conversely, have more – much more. The previously illustrated differences in resources that differing tax bases provide, sometimes within a single school district, lead to the types of educational atrocities that Jonathan Kozol describes in his 1991 work *Savage Inequalities*. While there are some that would argue that the alarms sounded by Kozol and others are limited to relatively few examples, it can also be argued that if there is even one school in America, the richest nation on earth, with raw sewage running across its playground, it is the stuff of national scandal.

Fortunately, there are alternatives to property taxes, such as individual income taxes, corporate income taxes, wealth taxes, value-added taxes, and expenditure taxes. One promising alternative to property tax would be the federal income tax, which now accounts for over 40 percent of the federal budget. Federal income tax is described by Joseph Peckman, of the Brookings Institute, as "the fairest and most productive source of revenue" among the nation's federal and state taxes (1977). Our point here is not to debate the merits of the various tax strategies, but rather to suggest that there are several alternatives to the presently inequitable system. There are three key steps to changing the funding paradigm for American education. The first step is attitudinal and the second two are logistical.

The first necessary change is in the area of purpose. As early as 1974, management guru Peter Drucker suggested that "getting one's business right" was more than a philosophical exercise, it was a critical question of survival. Drucker is famous for asking companies and corporations the question: "What business are you in?" As elementary as this sounds, it is a critical concept that some major industries and massive bureaucracies have failed to address. The classic example of an industry missing its real purpose is the American railroad system.

Not Quite Working on the Railroad

Americans traveling in either Europe or Asia cannot help but be struck by the quality of rail transportation found there. In both areas of the world, high-speed trains move large numbers of people long distances, quickly, safely, and economically. Japan's bullet trains connect Tokyo with most of the other major Japanese cities, moving passengers at 300Km/H. Europe's Eurail System connects France, Belgium, Germany, Italy, Norway,

Spain, and Sweden with high-speed trains also traveling up to 300Km/H, roughly 186 miles per hour.

In contrast, America's Amtrak, which has been plagued with a series of accidents, is using a deteriorating system of lines that suffer from poor or no maintenance, and, as of July 30, 2002, operate at low speeds, which they will continue to do for the foreseeable future. You might well ask, "How can this be?" How could the world's leading industrial country, in an era of energy crisis and ecological concern, have one of the world's most obsolete and dysfunctional rail systems? The answer lies in not knowing one's business.

Railroads in America got off, literally, to a slow start. In 1829, the first train on American tracks was pulled by a British-made locomotive at a mere ten miles per hour. During the 1830s, railroads began to catch on, despite opposition from canal and turnpike promoters and leery ministers who described the steam engine as a "device of Satan to lead immortal souls to Hell" (Readers Digest Association, 1975). At first, trains were used as a means of transporting freight between canals and natural waterways. The first major expansion of the rail network came in 1854 when Erastus Corning established the first railroad system, the New York Central, by merging several smaller lines. Rail expansion continued during the 19th century, with the transportation of both supplies and troops playing a significant role during the American Civil War. After six years of intense labor, the first transcontinental rail link was completed in 1869, and by 1883 four rail routes connected the east and west coasts of the United States.

As part of the incentive for the Union Pacific and Central Pacific railroad companies to undertake the monumental task of connecting America's coasts with rails, they were given alternating sections of land on both sides of the lines they built. The acquisition of vast tracts of land immediately put the railroads into the real estate business. Representatives of the rail companies traveled the world to lure immigrants to the American West with promises of cheap farmland and cheap rail transport of farm products to market. Hundreds of thousands of immigrants came west establishing farms and building factories, mines, and towns on the once open plains.

The high point for American railroads came in 1916, when 254 thousand miles of track carried 77 percent of the nations freight and 98 percent of its passengers. That same year, the developing automobile industry pressured Congress to pass the first grant-in-aid for highway construction. The growth of the auto industry, along with the development of bus transportation and the beginning of aviation, challenged the dominance of the railroads. Just as the canal and turnpike developers had resisted the development of railroads, the railroaders now began to lobby against the development of highways. Instead of utilizing these new technologies to supplement their business of moving people and freight, the railroads resisted them and unsuccessfully tried to compete with them.

By the 1970s, the rails were carrying less than 40 percent of America's freight and less than 1 percent of the intercity travelers. The federal government tried to sustain the viability of rail transportation with the creation of the National Railroad Passenger Corporation to run the 150-train Amtrak operations with the dismal results we have earlier noted. American railroads were once the leaders in the industrial growth of the United States. After loosing sight of the business, they deteriorated into an operation that today pales by comparison to the rail operations of the world's other industrial nations. America's schools suffered the same fate for the same reason.

A Shared Illusion

Like the leaders of the American railroad industry, the leaders of America's schools have never clearly identified what business they are in. Over the centuries of American schooling, millions of students and teachers have operated under the illusion that they were primarily involved in a process of education, while in reality, powerful forces were using them for quite different purposes. Countless legions of teachers (your authors included) entered American schoolrooms under the naïve impression that they were there to help students acquire the skills, values, information, and attitudes that would allow them to live productive and fulfilling lives. Many, including your authors, still see education offering students these possibilities. Unfortunately, those orchestrating the operation of schools have often had less lofty and more sinister purposes in mind. America's schools, organized and funded by the state, have most often been created for much more self-serving purposes.

As we have previously mentioned, schools were first established to promote Protestant morality and civic literacy. The curriculum in colonial schools was almost entirely religious in nature. Schools were designed to save souls and guide civic participation. They helped students learn to conform to religious and civic expectations. Early America was rural, agrarian, and predominantly White, Anglo-Saxon. This is not to say that there were not numbers of native peoples present, along with others brought to the new world as slaves, but as far as educational and civic purposes were concerned, these people did not exist.

As waves of immigrants arrived in America, schools were charged with the added function of socialization. While Americans loved to refer to their society as a "melting pot" the real name of the game was conformity. Schools became the engines of "Anglo conformity," instilling in immigrants the idea that their success depended heavily upon their ability to act, and even look, like the W.A.S.P. ideal. New immigrants refused to let their children speak anything but English, and millions changed their names to appear more WASP-like in origin.

As America passed through the 19th century, it went from a society of farmers and shopkeepers to one of industrialists and factory workers. The young country of farms and small towns evolved into to a developing nation of cities with slums and suburbs. In response, schools evolved as well.

The post-Civil war growth of industry demanded a new type of worker for the growing number of factories. Schools were charged with developing this labor force. Functionalists educators like Franklin Bobbitt were influenced by the writings of efficiency expert, F. W. Taylor, *The Principles of Scientific Management* (1911). Bobbitt and others developed curricular models that established links between industrial production and schooling. Children were referred to as the "raw materials" to be molded into the "finished products" – the model adults. What industry needed at this point was a well-educated elite to serve in management roles and the trained and compliant masses to do the heavy lifting. One of the new roles that school took on was that of sorting of children for the needs of industry and society.

By the time America entered World War II, this process of sorting had become institutionalized. Developmental theorists Piaget and Havighurst created models that helped in the sorting and routing of students, directing them to their appropriate "developmental tasks." Contrary to the educational ideals of independence and creativity, what factories really needed were complacent and compliant drones. Schools accommodated this need with the development of "life adjustment education," which had conformity as its goal. The purpose of this type of schooling was to promote adherence to the status quo.

In a sincere attempt to help children and young adults conform to existing social norms, they were exposed to activities with names such as; "learning an appropriate masculine and feminine role," "accepting one's physique," "desiring and achieving socially responsible behaviors," and accepting and adjusting to the physiological changes of middle age." This institutional madness was based on the idea that everyone had an appropriate role, and it was the school's duty to determine that function and track the students into predetermined career-oriented programs. In their 1946 book, *A Look at Our Schools: A Book for the Thinking Citizen*, Mort and Vincent rationalized this process, stating, "It is vain and wasteful to take a girl who would make a fine homemaker and try to fit her into the patterns of training that would make a lawyer, or to take a boy who would be successful in business and try to fit his training to that which produces doctors."

Schools to Save Society

By the end of the next decade, America's charge to its schools once again shifted, this time demanding that they save American society from the threat of Russian scientists. Like a windup toy, school bumped into America's embarrassment over Sputnik and charged off in yet another direction, this time to save America's Cold War pride. Within another decade, school was assigned yet another role, serving as the point-institution in the effort to desegregate American society. Rather than confronting discriminatory behavior in the realms of housing, employment, or services, America choose to start the battle for civil rights in the school yard.

The late 1960s and early 1970s offered a brief respite from school's constant series of non-educational distractions. Amidst the youth, counter-culture, and sexual revolutions, a generation of idealistic young people looked to schools as a place where they could make a significant impact and "change the world." Many were motivated not by the happy memories of their childhood school days, but by a sincere desire to replace the mind-numbing tedium of their own experiences with a more vital and exciting type of schooling. Toward that end, they began to "experiment" with concepts such as alternative schools, open classrooms, elective programs, schools without walls, team teaching, non-graded curriculums, alternative assessments, and interdisciplinary learning models. Some of these strategies produced impressive results, while others showed little significant achievement gains. The one unifying factor was that almost all of the alternative approaches were orchestrated by young, enthusiastic teachers who brought joy and excitement to their work and were motivated by a desire to improve learning. Overall, it made school an exciting place to attend. In the tradition of the old saying that "no good deed goes unpunished," this short-lived era came to a screeching halt with the end of the Vietnam War and the ensuing recession.

The mid-70s in America were marked by a conservative resurgence that swept the country. Polls indicated that people were tired of what they viewed as violence (both domestic and international), protest, and experimentation (both social and educational), and yearned for peace, stability, and what they referred to as "traditional values."

This last third of the 20th century marked the dawning of an era in which a small library of politically motivated reports critical of American education were written, and a seemingly limitless number of special interest groups entered the fray hoping to gain control of the school enterprise to promote their specialized agendas. From Coleman's 1966 *Equality of Educational Opportunity* to Bush's *No Child Left Behind*, American schools endured a constant series of critical assaults designed to promote political goals. The current crop of political action groups maneuvering for position using America's schools as their pulpits can be placed in ten general categories.

Among these groups are the Christian Coalition and the religious right, who hope to return prayer to schools and remove all anti-Christian ideas and any traces of secular humanism. The conservative think tanks want to establish a school curriculum that reflects Anglo-Saxon values and capitalistic ideologies. Neoconservatives hope to promote moral and social authority in schools and establish federal and state academic standards and measurements. The 2000 Republican Platform would require statewide testing programs with threatened takeovers of failing schools as a part of their vision of "compassionate conservatism." The Green Party wants to protect school children from the evils of consumerism and the resulting environmental damage caused by the present economic system. New Democrats would use state and national academic standards in schools to prepare students for participation in the global labor market. The Rainbow Coalition wants to use schools to eliminate gender and racial bias from society through the promotion of affirmative action programs. The National Organization of Women would utilize schools to eliminate gender bias and provide women with positive role models. Indiocentrics advocate schools for Native Americans under tribal control and provision of a non-Eurocentric curriculum. And finally, Afrocentric groups want funding for schools with curriculums based on African rather than European ways of thinking.

When reading this mind-numbing array of possibilities presented by groups both willing and eager to use America's school to promote their particular agenda, one cannot help but wonder if any of them really care about either students or education! After examining all of the functions historically attributed to schools and all of the current goals put forth by various action groups, the one item most conspicuously and consistently absent is real education. It could very well be that the main reason that schools today can't seem to effectively educate people is that they were never designed to do so in the first place and things are only getting worse. It seems that schools were never primarily about education. They were always about control. They controlled religious instruction, they controlled socialization, they controlled the sorting of workers for industry, and they controlled who had access to powerful knowledge. Schools controlled people by controlling information. Schools have had a monopoly on the dispensation of information and therefore on learning. Current political action groups know this well and are wrestling for dominance in this process. Schools have never had their business right.

Hold the Rhetoric, Pass the Amendment

While education may at one time have been considered an issue of local interest, at the dawn of the 21st century, American education is very much a matter of national interest. It can no longer be entrusted to a hit-and-miss system of local control. Education is clearly a matter of national prosperity and ultimately national survival.

To be truly effective, democratic forms of government require a well-educated and informed electorate who can wisely select their representatives and guide their actions. The armed services require well-educated and intelligent troops to effectively operate increasingly sophisticated weapons systems. Successful national and international businesses require a well-educated and skillful workforce that can develop and maintain competitive markets. Without the advantage of these educationally based resources, America will suffer in the arena of international competition.

Competing industrial nations hoping to become world powers will not be sending their most politically correct forces to either the marketplace or the battlefield; they will be sending their most competitive. They will not be hampered by a delusional vision of not leaving any of their students behind. Their clear goal will be to leave the United States behind. If we do not act quickly and decisively, these other nations will. Our only hope is to answer their challenges with our best and brightest graduates. In a very real sense, education is a most critical element in the area of national defense and economic survival. With this in mind, whose responsibility is it? Can a charge of this magnitude be left to individual school districts, with their own provincial vision of education and their varied and creative approaches to funding, any more than it can be left to special interest groups, each with its own self-serving agenda? Clearly it cannot!

Ideally the federal government should step up to the issue of American education and make it a legitimate, national priority rather than merely another part of election year rhetoric. A constitutional amendment could make education a national responsibility. In the alternative, the federal government could mandate a system in which the states are required to provide true equality of educational opportunity for all American students. In lieu of this type of decisive action on the part of the federal government, there is the possibility of states legislating educational funding reform on their own. In what would amount a ground-breaking move toward true democracy, states could place the issue of educational choice in the hands of parents and students, allowing them to directly influence the quality of their educational experience.

As we have indicated, this is presently nowhere near the case. The current economic disparity between school districts in any given state is significant, and the differences in economic resources between the states is profound. The question remains, why hasn't something been done to remedy this disgraceful situation? Perhaps part of the problem is that education has never adequately answered Peter Drucker's question.

Once we get back to the essential purpose of education, serving students, we can move ahead with the second paramount issue, funding. Proposals for school funding reform have typically fallen into three categories: a continuation of the current state-local funding formulas (in use throughout most of the country today), a full state funding model on a state-by-state basis, and a child-based funding model. Let us take a look at each of these alternatives to the present funding situation.

Several states have instituted a form of the full state funding plan with the intention of equalizing the educational funding levels within their boarders. Typically these plans put a ceiling on the expenditures of high-spending school districts while increasing the levels of aid to poor and low-spending districts. The net effect of this attempt has been significant in that it has proven unsatisfactory to almost all involved. In the case of the poor districts, the increases rarely seem adequate, while the resentment in the higher-spending districts grows, since they are limited in terms of the resources they are allowed to employ. Even if this strategy could be successfully implemented, allowing the states to equalize the funding formula within their boarders will do little overall good if the disparity in educational funding remains great from state to state. The net effect would be to change America from a country with tens of thousands of varying educational funding levels to a nation with fifty potentially different levels. True equality of educational opportunity would only be statistically closer.

A more effective alternative would be to establish a uniform, economic level of funding that could be administered on a per pupil basis for students no matter where they lived, a child-based funding system. Each American student would get a standard allotment of funding for each year of the educational experience. Assuming that the designated level of funding was adequate to ensure a quality education, this process would achieve the long-time goal of equality of educational opportunity. A second and critical part of this formula is determining where the funding should be spent.

What Are the Options?

While there are probably an infinite number of alternatives to the present educational funding formula, there are three general categories that represent a significant shift in the funding paradigm. They are full state funding of public schools, shared state-local funding of public schools, and child-based funding. Let us briefly examine the characteristics associated with each of these three alternatives.

Most full state funding programs would take control of spending for public education from the local school districts and give it to the state. This would result in central control of education within each state and help to equalize expenditures across districts. It could also be used to establish a statewide collective bargaining system for the uniform payment of all educational employees and uniform staffing ratios. The local property tax would remain as a part of the funding system, but the ability of the local districts to tax would be closely regulated and restricted by the state. User fees could be imposed by the local schools to cover the cost of items not funded by the state. While interesting, this plan has a number of drawbacks.

Foremost among the problems associated with full state funding is the fact that, while an equal amount of funding would be allocated to each district by the state, the local districts would still make the distribution decisions. Any concerns about the curricular knowledge or management skills of the local district boards would still exist. The second problem is one of teacher allegiance. Under full state funding, the efforts to equalize expenditures could lead to collective bargaining at the state rather than the local level. Teachers and other district staff would likely view themselves as state rather than district employees and place their allegiance with the source of their income. Finally there is the problem of overall effect. One of the main motivations of educational funding reform is to equalize the opportunity for educational quality for all American students. The full state funding plan would move the country in that direction, but still leave the nation with fifty potentially different approaches to the central issue.

A second alternative is the shared state-local funding option. This plan continues to place the major funding decisions at the discretion of the local boards and administration. The major difference between this plan and full state funding is that shared state-local funding would place a considerable amount of discretion in the hands of the local taxpayers and school boards. As in the present system, local boards would have the ability to determine which students received what services and to what degree. Under the shared state-local funding option, local districts would continue to receive major amounts of funding from local sources and maintain control over local policies and practices. Collective bargaining agreements would likely remain a local and individualized issue. While there would be uniformity in per-pupil funding allocations within districts, there would still be the possibility of wide variation between districts. In short, if the goal is true equality of educational opportunity, little has been accomplished in this scenario. A third possibility does, however, represent a substantial alternative.

The third significant alternative to the present model of educational funding is child-based funding. In the spirit of the classic American concept that education is the responsibility of the parents, child-based funding places the educational resources in the hands of parents. The mechanism for implementing child-based funding can be accomplished through vouchers and/or tax credits. This model is essentially a uniform, national, tuition allowance allocated to the parent or guardian of each student to be utilized in the educational option of their choice. The tuition allowance could be issued by the federal government to the family of each child. From there it would be presented to the learning institution of the family's choice. The educational agency would then present the materials to the government for redemption. An alternative, given the current technology available, would be to simply have the educational institution electronically present the government with student verification data and then collect tuition with a minimal exchange of physical paperwork. The source of the funding could be tied to a combination of state and/or federal income tax, with subsidy programs designed to assist low-income households.

Parents and students would have a variety of choices to make concerning the school of their choice, but little choice in terms of the level of spending since the tuition allowance rate would be standardized. In the case of handicapped students, low achievers, and the gifted, additional funding could be made available through special category vouchers. The clear advantage of the educational tuition allowance model is that its central purpose is to help the student, rather than the school or community. Students and their parents would have the ability to select schools on the basis of quality, rather than being assigned to a district and school on the basis of where they live.

Some of the previous proposals for the use of vouchers have suggested that they be used only in private schools. This almost always prompts a discussion concerning the appropriateness of using tax funding for private or parochial education. For some it is clearly a separation of church and state issue. Would the use of public funds to pay for private education be constitutionally permissible? While this question is often posed concerning the funding of K-12 education, it is a moot point for higher education in that tax dollars have been used for private higher educational enterprises for decades in the form of student loans, scholarships, and grants. The funding question should be resolved by making the proposed educational tuition allowance applicable to all qualified educational enterprises, either public or private. Keeping in mind that our overall goal is to improve education, not to save schools, let us take a look at the educational possibilities of the future.

Management consultant Steven Covey identifies the concept of "beginning with the end in mind" as one of the practices of highly effective people (Covey, 1989). Being mindful of the previously mentioned tendency to reform education by tinkering with schools, we believe that it is essential to consider a paradigm that will first and foremost meet the needs of education. If the goal is to educate rather than "school" students, then the results should be measured in terms of outcomes. The evaluation must be made in terms of verifiable accomplishment rather than hours of seat time.

The time-honored method of measuring academic accomplishment is the cognitive recall examination. Simply stated it is a written or oral process by which students are given the opportunity to demonstrate through recall the number of facts and processes that they have learned. Despite its popularity and long history of usage, the examination process has a number of shortcomings that could bear improvement. That however is a topic for another discussion. For the purposes of this process, we will accept the standardized cognitive recall examination as one measure of educational accomplishment.

The purpose of a nationwide and equitable educational system is to give every student an equal opportunity to learn and develop the academic skills necessary to succeed in the workforce, remain a life-long learner, and become an active member in our participatory democracy. While the accomplishment of all three goals will take a lifetime to evaluate, the accomplishment of the academic portion can be estimated through the use of standardized examinations. Instruments like the present Iowa Test of Basic Skills (Iowa Basics) or the California Test of Basic Skills (CTBS) could be easily developed, agreed upon, and administered on a nationwide basis. The development of the exam would, without doubt, be the subject of intense discussion, and the exam itself would, of necessity, need to be constantly revised and updated. Yet, if fairly and consistently administered and evaluated by an independent agency, these examinations could establish an accurate bank of base-line data indicating the overall efficiency of a variety of educational options.

The evaluation process could be divided into two basic types of exams, subject tests and synthesis tests. The subject tests would be administered at the end of each subject or interdisciplinary year. A student would, for example, complete the study of basic arithmetic or reading and take the corresponding examination to verify competency. If the exam was successful, the student would move on to another area of study. If not, the student would be allowed to study, attend class, and retake the exam at a later time. Students would be allowed to challenge any of the subject competency exams at any time. There would be no need to attend coursework for subject areas that were mastered independently. Learners would also have the option to develop competency through the use of tutors and/or individualized instruction. Students who entered the educational process knowing how to read would not have to patiently stand by while their fellow students caught up. They would challenge specific academic requirements throughout their academic careers in much the same way that college students satisfy graduation requirements. Periodic examinations of synthesis could be administered at ages six, ten, fourteen, and eighteen to measure the student's ability to understand and utilize the interactions and connections between and among the subject areas.

In much the same way that professional schools issue grades as an indication of readiness for state board or bar certification, schools could issue grades to students for each section of instruction. However, it would be the national examination for both subjects and synthesis sections that would verify successful completion of the activity. Educational providers would have the opportunity to compare the grades that they issued for instruction with the results of the national examinations then adjust for grade inflation and other potential inconsistencies.

As long as the national testing agencies were not affiliated with any of the organizations that they monitored and were subject to frequent auditing, the public could be assured that the results were dependable and accurate. Keep in mind the "end" we spoke of earlier. In this model, the goal of education is mastery and competency demonstrated through examination. The means utilized to achieve mastery is of significance only to the student. The overall goal in this paradigm is the product, not the process. One issue remaining is the scope of this enterprise.

Throughout the 20th century school has been a thirteen-year odyssey (K-12) consisting of approximately fifteen thousand hours of seat time. During this same century the total body of human knowledge doubled countless times. Present estimates are that the doubling rate is now every thirteen months. In terms of education, this leaves us with two uncomfortable possibilities. Either we have learned to deliver information much more effectively and much more rapidly than we did in the past, or students have been falling behind at roughly the same rate as the information deluge has pressed forward.

The obvious conclusion is that greater amounts of information require more educational time. We need to begin the education process at an earlier age and make it available on a year-round basis. In the mid 1940s, three National Education Association reports, *Education for All American Youth (1944), Educational Services for Children (1945),* and *Education for All American Children (1948),* recommended schooling for all children and youth starting at the age of three. While the timing may not have been correct for this change in the 1940s, it is certainly now long overdue. With the advent of the working family (both parents employed) and the single-parent family (a single working parent), pre-school children commonly wind up in some type of daycare facility. The overall quality of daycare providers varies greatly, and the educational benefit afforded by these environments is anybody's guess. Providing the previously labeled "pre-school population" with real educational opportunities would not only offer a sounder environment for their care, but also extend their learning experience where it is clearly needed. The second part of this equation is the extension of the educational calendar.

Education is possibly the only multi-billion dollar industry to shut down 25 percent of the time for reasons that no one can clearly identify. As we have discussed previously, the use of the agrarian calendar in the world of education is as outdated as the horse-drawn plows that were once used for farming. The post-industrial world demands an educational setting that is available to learners on a year-round basis. The concept of consumer friendliness must make its way into the world of education.

We have known for at least a century that all students do not learn at the same pace. Despite our best efforts to operate schools with factory-like uniformity, we have come to understand that educationally, at least, one size does not fit all. Despite all of the heated debate over the concept of reading-readiness, we have been forced to realize that students learn to read when they are ready – and not before. A year-round calendar could give students the option to take advantage of instruction at a pace set by students and their parents. Students could take time off for family vacations, educational travel, or simply to recover from an exhausting academic schedule. Voucher support would resume as soon as the student continued with their education. The flexibility of a year-round calendar with subjects offered on a rotational schedule would allow students the option of moving forward in their educational journey as quickly or as leisurely as they wished. They could learn when they were ready.

A year-round calendar with time off for vacations and holidays, along with a starting age of three years old would result in an educational experience lasting 23,076 hours, or an additional 65 percent more instructional time than is currently the case. This is not to imply that more is necessarily better. As is too often the case, more of the wrong thing can actually make matters worse. So the question arises, how do we evaluate this new model to determine its efficiency? In other words, how do we know if these educational strategies work?

Is It Working Yet?

One of the reasons this is such an interesting question is the historical lack of accountability in education. For as long as they have existed, schools have not been held responsible for their efficiency or effectiveness in any real sense. When the authors of this book have asked administrators in high schools around the world how effective their schools were, they invariably answered, "Excellent." When pressed to give evidence of this excellent status, administrators most commonly cited the number of their students that they sent on to college after graduation. In the best of circumstances, this number was approximately 30 percent of the school's graduating class. If pressed to account for the success of the other 70 percent of the class, principals typically responded that they were not sure, but believed that the students were all doing fine. The sad fact is that the administrators, in reality, had no idea! After their senior year, the graduates of most high schools could be abducted by aliens from another planet without their former teachers and administrators having any knowledge of the incident. There is no follow-up. One of the unique qualities of the schooling industry is that the workers have absolutely no responsibility for the outcome of their labor. When failure does become apparent, it is the student who is blamed. Schools traditionally blame their victims, and this cannot be allowed to continue.

While it is true that the responsibility issue has not gone totally un-noticed, and efforts such as the accountability movement of the 1980s have made efforts to address the problem, they have been largely ineffective as evidenced by the current state of crisis. True accountability must be firmly connected to the outcome of the process. Early educational experiences must be judged on the basis of how well students do in the ensuing levels of education. Do students emerge from the early years of education ready to read, write, and compute at a level that will ensure success in future learning enterprises? Can students who receive passing grades in reading, writing, and mathematics actually perform in these academic skills? The same standard must be applied at the upper levels of education.

While college admission rates are interesting, it is college completion rates that result in economic productivity. It is wonderful that 30 percent of a graduating class is admitted to college, but how many of them are equipped to graduate from college? In addition to the college-bound, the other 70 percent of high school graduates should be tracked to determine their rate of continuing education and also their educational success rates. Finally, it would be appropriate for an institution to keep track of the types of jobs that its graduates acquired and kept. This final piece of data would give a more complete picture of the overall effectiveness of a learning strategy. Like any other skilled workers, educators should be held accountable for their productivity. If educators assign a passing grade, it should assure the student and their parents that the student is capable of passing an examination and actually performing the related skill. The question that many are asking themselves at this point is, "Why should educators do any of this?"

The answer is simple: choice. Students should have the option to spend their educational tuition allowance in the educational setting of their choice. Students should no longer be held captive by school zoning based on where they happen to live. Educational enrollment should no longer be a matter of default placement. Students must have the option to shop for quality. For most, that decision will be largely based on proven results. All students will have the same resource base to fund their education. Students will not be inclined to waste their time and money on an institution or provider with a poor track record when there are others who are competent and eager to earn their business.

In short order, educational providers will realize that the key to their success and survival is the ability to attract students to their programs. Poor quality providers will be "terminally evaluated" by students who vote with their feet and take their vouchers elsewhere. Learning centers that issue grades that do not correspond with the student's ability to pass exams will be quickly exposed as inefficient. Quality providers will openly advertise their test results and market their programs to prospective students. With test results verified by independent testing agencies and accurate records of the success rates of previous graduates, learning institutions will have the ability to give new meaning to the phrase "quality education." Those who wish to learn will have opportunities to learn as quickly and efficiently as they would like. There will also be new opportunities for those who do not wish to further their education.

The noble experiment of universal education has historically had one serious flaw. There are some students who simply do not wish to be educated. In many cases, these individuals demonstrate their lack of enthusiasm for the education process on a daily basis by interrupting the work of their teachers and the learning process of their classmates. The sad fact about compulsory universal schooling is that, in spite of our best efforts, it has failed. While is it possible, in dire situations, to force-feed people, it is not possible to force-educate them. While school attendance may have been mandatory, learning has always been optional. Those who refuse to learn have, too often, been a hindrance to those who want to learn.

The age limits for mandatory attendance vary from state to state, as do the processes for monitoring truancy. Due to state funding formulas based on the average number of students in attendance, schools have been reluctant to terminate students' enrollments for fear of losing the corresponding funding. Since schools have not been traditionally held accountable for a student's lack of accomplishment or productivity, there has been little incentive to remove a non-productive or disruptive student who is generating funding, in spite of the fact that they are also hindering the education of other students. In an educational paradigm based on accomplishment this would change.

In a new paradigm, education could be recognized as a life-long activity, but attendance would be mandatory only between the ages of three and twelve. During this period, funding in the form of the educational tuition allowance (voucher) would be guaranteed. As long as a student was enrolled and attending, the educational provider could apply for the tuition allowance. After the age of twelve, continued governmental support would be dependent upon accomplishment. If the student continued to participate in educational activities and demonstrate success on the subject competency exams, funding would continue. If success was not evident, the student would be given a finite period of time to remediate his or her deficiencies. If improvement in the form of successful examinations were not demonstrated, funding would cease. Students no longer interested in furthering their education would now be faced with alternative opportunities. The primary alternative is an organization of historical significance, whose time has come again.

In 1932, America was in the grip of a major depression. Unemployment and economic chaos was rampant. Newly elected President Franklin Roosevelt set about creating an organization that would resolve two of the nation's lingering problems: unemployment and the destruction of its natural resources. In March of 1933, Roosevelt called the 73rd Congress into Emergency Session to consider Senate Bill 5.598, the Emergency Conservation Work (ECW) Act, more commonly known as the Civilian Conservation Corps (CCC). The bill went through both houses of Congress and was signed on March 31, 1933. With this single bill, Congress and the president eventually put over three million young men to work and made enormous strides to halt the destruction and erosion of America's natural resources. A judge in Chicago stated that he believed that the CCC was responsible for a 55 percent reduction in crime among young men in that city. Decades before the term "ecology" entered the American lexicon, work was begun that saved two of America's invaluable natural resources.

Today we are faced with similar demands. Awareness of the need to preserve and maintain America's ecological resources has never been higher, and the need to provide young citizens with service options and employment opportunities has never been greater. Creation of a civic organization similar to the CCC could, today, serve as an alternative activity for students between the ages of twelve and eighteen who were not currently interested in educational opportunities. After a year of paid service in the CCC, students would be allowed to re-apply for admission to an educational institution, where their productivity would again determine continued participation. Unlike the depression-era CCC, with its resident camps in remote locations, the modern version could be local or regional so that participants could remain at home during their service opportunity. Students who chose to remain in the conservation corps would have the opportunity to learn craft and technical skills that could lead to employment opportunities and be further developed in trade and technical schools. The net result of this type of program would be to give young men and women who are not interested in formal academic development the opportunity to learn and perform meaningful service in a hands-on setting. It would also free teachers and serious academic students from the distraction of disruptive classmates.

Avoiding the Paralyzing Fear of Change

One of the most common questions asked of recent graduates from educational graduate programs is, "What do we need to do to fix education?" What those posing the question are hoping for is a simple, one-step solution. When the graduate launches into an involved reform process, as we have in this book, the listener's eyes begin to glaze over. The process of change begins to appear more frightening than the continued crisis. In many instances, people are more comfortable with continued inefficiency than they are with the prospect of uncertainty that comes with the change process.

The sad reality in a world of exponential change is that some people will always be left behind. During the space race of the 1960s, there were voices in America that strenuously objected to spending money on putting a person on the moon while there were still needy people here on earth. If America had hesitated at that time, exploring space would still be a far-off dream. Likewise, if we wait for optimum conditions to be in place before restructuring education, we will, in all likelihood, never act. Amidst the present barrage of political rhetoric, Americans are confusing the concepts of equality of educational opportunity with equality of educational outcomes. Equality of educational outcomes is no more possible than the Lake Woebegone claim that everyone can be above average. The model we suggest is based in a fervent belief in the possibility of a truly equal educational opportunity for all Americans.

While the possibility of changing a colossal institution such as America's schools seems potentially overwhelming, there is precedence for activity of this magnitude. In the next chapter we will examine the other gigantic American trusts and monopolies that have been dramatically restructured.

High Tech Warriors

The Army high tech prototype uniform, set for the year 2010, is part of a $15 billion Future Combat System project that will indeed be futuristic. Weighing only 50 pounds, the "Scorpion ensemble" will be wired to monitor vital signs, and to link the combatant to a host of satellites, robots, and unmanned aircraft. The suit comes with self-tightening tourniquets, body armor, and cartridges to hold extra batteries and circuits.

The high-tech helmet will hold tiny cameras to note objects in the dark or behind bushes. Images will be projected onto semi-transparent screens on the faceplate. Infrared cameras for seeing through smoke, global positioning maps, and laser tags to identify "friendlies" will aid in ordering aircraft strikes. Voice recognition and sleeve controls will make up the ensemble.

The Scorpion suit will have open architecture so that various devises can be swapped as technology advances. On the horizon? Chameleon-like camouflage suites, rifles that fire "air-burst" grenades for reaching around corners in combat, and personal robots to minimize risks.

Source: Michael Reagan, Associate Press, June 7, 2003.

Chapter Seven

After the Funding Monopoly is Busted

> It is entirely appropriate in a democracy for
> parents and students to have a significant choice
> in how they become educated.

A comment and a question are often heard when the discussion turns to the restructuring of American education. The comment: "Public schooling in America is too well-ingrained an institution to ever be changed." The question: "Is there really any viable alternative to the present system?"

In this chapter we will address both issues. American public education has not remained in place, unchanged, for so long because it is a system that works. Public schools in America are ingrained because they have a monopoly on educational funding. There are a number of viable alternatives to the public school system that demonstrate degrees of success, despite the fact that they have been privately funded. Can the public education system ever be changed? Absolutely! As we will show, public schools would be far from the first giant American monopoly to be faced with the choice of efficiency or obsolescence.

Monopolies and Trusts

A monopoly is defined as the exclusive control of a commodity or service. Monopolies allow a company or corporation to artificially manipulate activity levels and fix prices. Historically, monopoly has been a "dirty word" in the American vocabulary, flying in the face of the democratic ideal of equality of economic opportunity. The concept of monopoly is often associated with trusts: corporations who hold monopoly powers within their business or industry. Longstanding opposition to this type of unfair restriction is most often referenced in connection with the Sherman Anti-Trust Act of 1890, the Clayton Anti-Trust Act of 1914, and the leadership of "trust busting" presidents Theodore Roosevelt and William Taft. During their presidencies, legislation was enacted that restricted the unfair practices of corporate giants like Standard Oil and American Tobacco.

The motivation for this type of legislation traces its roots to the development of Jacksonian Democracy. As early as 1837, the U.S. Supreme Court issued a decision that clearly promoted the idea of business competition and the elimination of monopolies. In 1835, Justice John Marshall died and Andrew Jackson replaced him with Roger Taney, who became the fifth Chief Justice of the U.S. Supreme Court. Taney, unlike his predecessor, was in favor of business competition and opposed monopolies. In Charles River Bridge v. Warren River Bridge, the Taney court indicated that the key to democracy was the expansion of economic opportunity. The court held that this could not occur if established corporations maintained monopolies that were allowed to choke off competitive efforts by newer companies. The record of anti-trust action continued throughout the 18th, 19th, and 20th centuries. During the presidency of Theodore Roosevelt there were forty-four anti-trust suits, followed by ninety more during the Taft administration. This process remained active throughout the remainder of the 20th century.

One of the most readily recognized monopolies to be dismantled during the 20th century was American Telephone and Telegraph. During the 106 years between Alexander Graham Bell's invention of the telephone and the anti-trust action of 1982, Bell Telephone had a virtual monopoly on telephone communications in the United States. If you wanted telephone service, there was only one option. Despite the seven years of holding action on the part of AT&T and a noteworthy display of bad attitude on the part of their employees after the decision was rendered, the corporate giant finally agreed to sell off 66 percent of its assets. The result has been a revitalized and competitive communications industry that offers consumers an almost endless array of options at competitive rates. While the telephone was a technological innovation that became an essential element of modern life, America has other major institutions that have a longer history in providing even more time-honored necessities.

America's postal delivery system and its school system are two examples of essential services that date back to the time of the founding of the country. Both are time-honored institutions providing indispensable service that at some points in their histories have been considered quite effective and at others damned as illustrations of inefficiency. The most notable difference between the two is the degree to which one has been allowed to maintain a monopoly.

Thirty-two years after Jamestown passed the Old Deluder Satan Act, which required every Colonial town to have a school, Richard Fairbank's tavern in Boston was named the first repository for overseas mail. In 1775, the Continental Congress named Benjamin Franklin the first Postmaster General. Over the next 191 years, the Post Office grew into an enormous bureaucracy that made few adjustments to accommodate developing

189

technologies. In 1838, Congress designated the railroads as postal routes. In 1911, mail was carried by airplane between Garden City and Minneola, New York. By 1935, trans-Pacific mail service was established, followed by trans-Atlantic service in 1939. While these few technological innovations were incorporated into the basic system of delivering mail, the essential process remained unchanged.

In 1966, the long-standing inability of the Post Office Department to respond to changing times, changing conditions, and evolving paradigms reached critical mass. One of its largest hubs, the Chicago Post Office, ground to a virtual halt in a logjam of mail. At a congressional hearing in 1967, Oklahoma Congressman Tom Steed, chairman of the House Appropriations Subcommittee on Treasury-Post Office, accused Postmaster General Lawrence O'Brien of having "a staggering amount of 'no control' in terms of the duties he had to perform." The sad reality was that this "total lack of control" on the part of the Postmaster General was largely due to the fact that, in spite of a skyrocketing volume of mail, the Postal Service was, with the possible exception of the use of ZIP Codes, handling mail in essentially the same manner that it had for the previous one hundred years! This major crisis eventually led to the passage of Public Law 91-375 in 1970 under which the Post Office Department was transformed into the United States Postal Service, an independent establishment of the executive branch of the Government of the United States.

Opportunities for Competition

Long before the postal meltdown of 1966, farsighted entrepreneurs saw opportunities to fill the voids left by inadequate postal service. In 1907, James E. Casey borrowed $100 from a friend and established the American Messenger Company in Seattle, Washington. In the early days, the company made most of its local deliveries on foot, using bicycles for longer trips. Early on, Casey established a strict policy of customer courtesy, reliability, round the clock service, and low rates, qualities some would say are still lacking in the USPS. In 1919 the American Messenger Company expanded its service to Oakland, California, and changed its name to United Parcel Service. During this time, the company embraced technological innovations to improve efficiency. In 1924, UPS was the first to use a conveyor belt to expedite the handling of packages.

As is the case with any business successfully competing in the free market, UPS was forced to adjust to changing conditions. With the increasing usage of the telephone and automobile, the need for messenger services began to diminish. In response, UPS began to focus on package delivery, and, for two years, the company's largest client was the U.S. Post Office. UPS delivered all of the special delivery mail entering Seattle. Building on this success, in the 1950s, UPS began to acquire "common carrier" rights to deliver packages between all customers, both private and commercial. This decision placed UPS in direct competition with the U.S. Postal Service and on questionable ground with the Interstate Commerce Commission. UPS began its expansion by establishing common carrier operations in cities where authorization from the state commerce commission or the ICC was not required. At the same time they sought to expand their operating authority in the state of California. This action prompted a series of protracted legal battles before regulatory commissions and courts. The goal of UPS was simply to operate in areas where there was a demand for its unique services.

Over the next thirty years, UPS pursued more than one hundred applications for additional operating authority. It took three decades of work for UPS to finally obtain authorization to ship packages freely in all forty-eight contiguous states. Like its main competition the Postal Service, UPS finally had the right to serve every address in the United States. A private company that refused to be intimidated by a monolithic, governmental bureaucracy and monopolistic regulations introduced an element of competition into a field that historically had none. In retrospect, it would be hard to argue that this competition has not only improved package delivery efficiency, but has also forced the USPS to update and modernize its operations.

One year before the postal meltdown of 1966, a Yale undergraduate by the name of Fredrick W. Smith wrote a term paper analyzing the passenger routing systems that were used by most of the airfreight shippers of the day. Smith's position in the paper was that the existing systems, designed for moving passengers, were economically inadequate; what was needed was a system specifically designed to move airfreight effectively and efficiently. He believed that this was particularly important in the shipment of time-sensitive materials such as medicines, computer parts, and electronics.

After serving in the military, Smith bought Arkansas Aviation Sales in August of 1971 and began to research the issue of package delivery systems. His goal was to establish a process that would allow him to deliver packages and other airfreight within a day or two, rather than the extended periods that were the norm. This goal was the concept that led to the creation of Federal Express.

Federal Express, incorporated in 1971, officially began operations in 1973 with a fleet of fourteen small aircraft operating out of the Memphis International Airport. During their first night of operation, FedEx delivered 186 packages to twenty-five U.S. cities.

In 1974, FedEx launched a $150,000 media advertising campaign using the slogan, "Federal Express – A Whole New Airline for Packages Only." After their first commercial hit the airways, the number of packages sent rose from three thousand per night to ten thousand. By November of

1988, the company was consistently moving ten thousand packages every night.

In February of 1989, FedEx went international by acquiring Tiger International Inc. (Flying Tigers). By August of that year, FedEx was the world's largest full-service, all-cargo airline. In 1995, they acquired Evergreen International Airlines and expanded their service area even further. The development and success of Federal Express has been accompanied by their willingness to change and innovate. FedEx was the first company dedicated to overnight package delivery, the first to introduce the overnight letter, the first to offer 10:30 a.m. next day delivery and Saturday delivery, and the first in their industry to offer money-back guarantees and free proof of performance services. As was the case with UPS, FedEx was willing to innovate and adopt new paradigms of operation as times and markets changed and evolved. The FedEx impact on the operation of the U.S. Postal Service is in many ways similar to that of UPS. Both companies forced competition into an arena that had formerly been dominated by a restrictive monopoly.

An Example of Adaptation

Despite the example of the Postal Service and its resistance to change, there are positive examples of huge governmental institutions that have modified their mode of operation to meet the changing needs of society and function at a high level of efficiency. A classic of example of change to meet emerging conditions is the United States military. The American armed services is a massive organization that has demonstrated the ability to respond to the two greatest challenges facing sustainable enterprise: appropriate use of emerging technology, and adaptation to changing social conditions. Both of these critical qualities were identified and discussed early in the last century.

During the Great Depression, the administration of Herbert Hoover commissioned sociologist William Fielding Ogburn to study the relationship between rapidly growing technological development and the ability of society to respond to the resulting changes. In his book, *Social Change*, Ogburn presented his theory of "Culture Lag," describing the growth rate of technology as approaching exponential while the ability of society to respond was linear and reactive. Ogburn noted that as technology continued to rapidly develop, society continued to respond slowly, and the gap in reaction time (or Culture Lag) continued to grow. The only means of reducing the lag between technological development and social adaptation was through anticipatory future planning. Individuals and organizations must either anticipate and plan for technological change or continue to fall further behind. Historically few private organizations have demonstrated the ability to respond to technological change as well as the U.S. military.

In its roughly three hundred year history, the armed forces of the United States has gone from reliance on muzzle-loading black-powder weapons to remote-controlled, unmanned, aircraft and laser-guided smart bombs and missiles. Nearly every modern weapons system reflects the latest in computer technology. Historically, the American military has been at the forefront of research in the area of weapons development. Many of the technological innovations that we take for granted in the 21st century were originally developed for military use. The triage process for managing massive medical emergencies, the use of helicopters for medical evacuation, the large scale development of antibiotics, the development of radar and television, wireless radio communication, jet and rocket propulsion, and the development of nuclear energy all started as military research projects. Whether you support or condemn the uses that politicians have historically made of the American military complex; it is impossible to ignore their record of technological development and adaptation. Admittedly, the success or failure of a military operation is blatantly more obvious than the success or failure of an enterprise like public education. Unlike schools, where failure is evident in society only years after the fact, it is painfully obvious when an armed force goes to war and fails to succeed. This is undoubtedly part of the greater motivation for change.

Until recently, the field of education has never faced any type of significant pressure to be accountable for its results. There has never been a truly compelling reason to enact substantive change. The earliest form of product delivery in education was the lecture. After centuries of use, the lecture is still the most revered form of information transferal. If the U.S. armed forces followed education's lead in embracing and utilizing technology, they would use rock-throwing slings to defend America from the threat of attack by weapons of mass destruction. This is not to imply that the military has not had its share of problems adapting to the use of technology. Historians often accuse the military of fighting today's wars using modern weapons and yesterday's tactics. America's Civil War was rife with examples of commanders using outdated Napoleonic field strategies against long-range modern rifles – with disastrous results. The point is the military was able to learn from its errors and adapt to changing conditions and evolving technologies. Education never has. One of the authors of this book first used a desktop computer as a learning tool at the War College in Columbus, Georgia, thirteen years before the first crude computer appeared in an American public school! As Ogburn's theory of change implies, it is the ability of a society or organization to respond to technology that significantly impacts its success. In addition to the ability to adapt to developing technology, the second area of critical development identified early in the 20th century was the need for appropriate adaptation to changing social conditions.

The issue of social adaptation was also identified during the Great Depression, this time by progressive educator, George Counts. Counts was concerned about the ability of institutions to reform their operations to meet the demands of changing conditions, especially during times of social unrest. Count's 1932 book *Dare the Schools Build a New Social Order?* challenged America's schools to lead in the area of social change rather than slowly reacting or totally ignoring the process. Clearly, education did not meet the challenge. One of the strengths of the American military is that it has historically done a much more effective job of responding to changing times and conditions.

As with most emerging nations, the military forces of the United States began as local militias organized for the defense of the colonies. As the need arose for larger military forces to deal with combative interactions with other nations, the armed services of the United States developed using the armed forces of Western Europe as models. By the time of the American Civil War, the armed forces of America shared all of the positive qualities, as well as the limitations, of the major combative forces of the day.

In the mid-1800s, the emerging field of sociology was debating the relative importance of the society verses that of the individual. America's armed services reflected the dominant thought of the day. Military units were drawn from regions of the country and bore names like the Wisconsin Infantry and the Maine Volunteers that clearly established their group origins. The services stressed patriotism and teamwork. *Esprit de corps* was based on common purpose and the common backgrounds of the soldiers. This sense of group cohesion and team unity in the military persisted through World War II. For instance, a well-known combat unit from this conflict, the

101st Airborne, was described by historian Steven Ambrose as a band of brothers.

As America entered the cultural revolution of the 1960s, with its corresponding shifts in personal awareness, the American military kept pace. With the new-age rise of the individual and the cultural admonition to "do your own thing," the military shifted from the old theme of unit identity to a new, more individualistic, theme urging soldiers to "Be all you can be." As this trend toward individualism and the emergence of the "me generation" continued in the 80s and 90s, military recruiters promised new recruits the opportunity to become "an Army of one."

The American military has also paid close attention to the country's attitudes toward the business of warfare. Prior to the 1950s, all military activities were conducted under the direction of the War Department. After World War II, it was correctly assumed that the public would be more inclined to provide funding for defense than they would for war, thus the name of the central organization was changed to the Defense Department.

By the end of the 20th century, the American military complex had become an all-volunteer organization of professionals and had made significant progress in the areas of ethnic integration, gender equity, and the acceptance of diverse social life-style groups. Largely due to its ability to adapt to changing times and conditions, the American military was able to maintain its effectiveness and America's position as the sole world superpower at the dawn of the 21st century. Despite the occasional My Lai and Tail Hook incidents, the American military organizations have been able to adapt to changing conditions and maintain their status as the world's leading military force. Unlike the Postal Service and America's schools the history of the American military indicates that large, bureaucratic, institutions can and do successfully change and develop over time.

If it is to be at all successful, the same descriptors must be applicable to the field of education. In a world of exponential change, there is no hope for out-dated monopolies that refuse to address rapidly emerging conditions. Institutions that refuse to face the realities of change become liabilities rather than assets. The public school monopoly, due to its lack of willingness to change and adapt, has become a liability.

America's Other Historic Monopoly

Roughly paralleling the development of the U.S. Postal Service, the American public school system has enjoyed a monopoly on educational funding that would be the envy of any corporate giant. American public schools, like pre-1982 AT&T and the early Postal Service, have a monopoly on education in the United States. While there are literally hundreds of alternative means of acquiring an education, it is only the public school system that is allowed to receive public financial support. By any definition this is a monopoly and should be subject to the same type of antitrust action responsible for reforming Ma Bell.

Alternatives to the public schools have been in operation for most of the two hundred year history of public education. They exist in the form of home schools, democratic and free schools, folk education institutions, Friends (Quaker) Schools, Krishnamurti Schools, Montessori Schools, Open Schools, Waldorf Schools, therapeutic schools, independent schools, private schools and Parochial Schools. There are literally dozens of alternatives to public schools that students and parents may employ to acquire an education. The problem centers on the issue of financing.

The present situation is tragically comical. There is only one educational system in America that qualifies for public support and, by all accounts, it is failing. There are dozens of alternatives to public schools that people find attractive and functional, however those who choose any form of education other than the public schools are forced to finance the venture on their own. At the same time they are taxed to support the system they seek to avoid. It is like telling consumers that they can do business with the phone company of their choice, but they must also pay Ma Bell for services they do not use. Send all of the packages you wish through UPS or FedEx, but you still owe postage to the USPS.

What we are advocating is an end to the stranglehold: American public school's monopoly on educational funding. It is long overdue and entirely appropriate in a democracy for parents and students to have choices in education. Our purpose in this chapter is to display and describe some of the infinite choices that exist in the realm of educational possibilities. This process will in no way be comprehensive in that the list of ways in which people may choose to become educated is in fact infinite, limited only by their imaginations. Rather, our intent is to inform the reader of areas for further exploration and to firmly establish that the American public school system is far from the only way to get an education.

Alternatives Unlimited

As we have stated before, there are literally unlimited alternatives to the American public school system of education. While it would be impossible to list and describe all of them, we have elected to concentrate on some of the most common examples of these alternatives.

Homeschooling

One of the fastest growing forms of alternative schooling in the United States is the homeschool. The homeschool movement developed rapidly during the 1990s, growing from an estimated 0.8 percent of the K-12 student population in 1994, to 1.4 percent by 1996. It is estimated that there were between 345,000 and 636,000 children between the ages of six and seventeen participating in some form of home-based education during this decade (Martin, 2000).

While often dismissed as a haven for Christian fundamentalists upset about the ban on prayer in public schools, this movement actually has a much broader base of support. Two of the movements closely associated with homeschooling are "unschooling" and "deschooling."

Unschooling was advocated by John Holt, author of *How Children Fail* (1964). In this attack on public education, Holt criticized what he described as a "tell them/test them" model of teaching, which convinced students that school was a meaningless place with meaningless questions, meaningless answers, and meaningless activities. In *How Children Fail*, Holt equated schools with jails where students bide their time waiting to get out and have the opportunity to express their more creative energies. According to Holt, survival in school required a process of passive compliance. Toward the end of his life Holt had completely given up on the concept of school reform and encouraged parents to educate their children at home. A current source for unschooling is Grace Llewellyn's *Teenage Liberation Handbook: How to Quit School and Get a Real Life and Education* (1997). Llewellyn's intent was to provide a guide to learning through personal experience and community opportunities for students and parents disenchanted with the traditional "cells and bells" model of public schooling.

Deschooling is based on the work of Ivan Illich, *Deschooling Society* (1970). Illich advocated deschooling as a means of ending the "one size fits all" model of public schooling, replacing it with a web of interest-based "learning communities" that would allow free access to knowledge. A recent book by Matt Hern, *Deschooling Our Lives* (1997), offered examples of ways for students to take control of their education and escape from what Illich called "the corrosive effects of compulsory schooling."

Further information on the topics of homeschooling, unschooling, and deschooling can be obtained at the Family Unschoolers Network (www.unschooling.org), and from the website for Home Education Magazine (www.unschooling.com), as well as Karl Bunday's School is Dead: Learn in Freedom website, and *What Do I Do on Monday* (1970) and *Freedom and Beyond* (1972) by John Holt.

Democratic and Free Schools

While there are many examples of the free school model, most associate the term with the English Summerhill School founded by A.S. Neill. In the years since the 1921 establishment of Summerhill, several variations on Neill's theme have emerged. In all cases, the driving goal is to establish a learning environment where students can become educated without the use of force and coercion commonly associated with traditional schooling, allowing children's natural curiosity to lead the learning process.

Many of the free schools are organized in a manner that allows them to also operate as democratic schools. These institutions function in the true sense of a democracy in that all parties involved have a voice in the decision-making process. Students and teachers have the ability to express their opinions concerning matters of school operation and governance. In some institutions, students and teachers have an equal vote in policy matters.

Examples of democratic and free schools include Play Mountain Place in Los Angles, the Albany Free School, the Children's Village School in Thailand, and the Sudbury Valley School. Further information about democratic and free schools can be found on the following website: http://www.PathsOfLearning.net/archives/freeschools2000.htm.

Folk Education

Folk education is defined by the Folk and People's Education Association as: "learning that happens when individuals and communities come together to celebrate culture and life in order to critically analyze challenging and especially oppressive situations, to build a knowledge base and to apply that knowledge to create alternative possibilities for the institutions in which we live and work." Folk education is a model primarily emphasizing education for adults and specifically targeting their political empowerment. It originated as a Scandinavian grassroots movement in the 1800s. By 1925, there were over three hundred thousand young Danes enrolled in folk schools that were not controlled by the government. These schools did not use grades, tests, or diplomas, and established a curriculum centered on the issues relevant to the lives of their students. Folk education is sometimes referred to as "radical adult education," "eco-teams," and "people's education." The goal of all of these variations is education for social change. A good source of information on folk education in the United States is the Folk and People's Education Association of America (http://www.peopleseducation.org). The association has a newsletter, a quarterly journal, and an annual conference.

Friends (Quaker) Schools

The Society of Friends was founded in 1648 by George Fox. Fox admonished his congregation in 1650 to "tremble at the word of the Lord," thus giving them the nickname Quakers. Persecuted by the established church in England, the Quakers fled to America where they were treated in much the same manner by the Puritans.

The Quakers have a long history of social activism and sound educational practice. As early as 1727, the Quakers demanded the abolition of slavery and provided the first educational opportunities for freed Blacks. Early on, Quaker education, which was known for its excellent academic quality, was made available to girls as well as the poor. Teachers in Quaker schools have always been given apprenticeship training, the first form of teacher education in America (Pulliam, 1987).

To this day, the goal of Quaker education is one of guiding students to "uncover their own leadings" through self-direction. There is an emphasis on personal and individual responsibility, working against human oppression, maintaining life-long learning, and establishing social justice. The student's role in Quaker schools is to be a responsible learner and community member. The teacher's role is "to make daily space for the inward journey of every student" (Palmer, 1998). One of the global goals of the Friends schools is "creating the world that ought to be."

Structurally Quaker schools look quite traditional, issuing grades, dividing students by grade level, with teachers who use traditional teaching methods. Nevertheless, they are quite unique in their use of meetings, queries, silence, and special conflict resolution techniques called "clearness committees."

One of the best current sources of information about Quaker ideas and ideals employed in education appears in the writings of Quaker Parker Palmer. Palmer's quest is to return spirituality to education. His popular book *The Courage to Teach* has caught the attention of many seeking alternatives to the present public school system and has even found support in traditional university schools of education. Other sources on Friends Schools include the Friends Council on Education (http://mathforum.com/fce/), and the Meeting School website (http://www.mv.com/ipusers/tms/).

Krishnamurti Schools

Krishnamurti schools are institutions designed to help students "learn about the totality, the wholeness of life." According to their founder, Jiddu Krishnamurti, they are places "where both the teacher and the taught explore not only the outer world, the world of knowledge, but also their own thinking, their own behavior." The schools are designed to be an oasis where students can learn in a holistic, sane, and intelligent manner.

All Krishnamurti schools are similar in their central purpose, with each individual school evolving in what is described as a "methodless" or "pathless" manner. Each school is seen as a "place where one learns the importance of knowledge and its limitations." Some Krishnamurti schools emphasize an academic focus, while others have a spiritual emphasis. Information about the Krishnamurti schools can be found on the Krishnamurti Information Network's Community website at the following address: http://www.kinfonet.org/Community/.

Montessori Schools

One of the best-known alternative forms of education in the United States is the Montessori school. The schools are based on the work of Maria Montessori, a pioneer in the field of education and the first woman to become a medical doctor in her native Italy. Dr. Montessori advocated a personal and progressive curriculum for children. While some Americans showed interest in the ideas of Montessori as early as 1911, rapid growth of the Montessori pre-schools for young children started in the 1970s.

Similar in purpose to Head Start and Title One programs, Montessori pre-schools are designed as skill-readiness programs to help prepare students for later schooling. In Montessori model schools, children are "trained" to identify and manipulate shapes, numbers, letters, and other symbols, as well as learning order, obedience, sharing, and various social skills. According to the American Montessori Society, "the aim of Montessori education is to foster competent, responsible, adaptive citizens who are lifelong learners and problem solvers." The importance of this type of quality pre-school education becomes more obvious as research continues to estimate that nearly one-half of all learning by humans occurs during the first six years of life.

As of 1997, there were over three thousand Montessori schools in the United States. The majority of these were private pre-schools, however, a significant change in the funding formula could result in a dramatic increase in Montessori charter institutions. For more information on the structure and philosophy of Montessori education, access the following sites: International Montessori Society (http://www.wdn.com/trust/ims/), American Montessori Society (http://www.amshq.org/), and North American Montessori Teacher's Association (http://www.montessori-namta.org/).

Open Schools (and Classrooms)

Since the mid 1960s, two basic approaches have been vying for dominance in the field of school curriculum. On one side, there are the perennialists and essentialists calling for a standardized subject matter, high academic standards, discipline oriented schools, and a no-nonsense basic education. This group traces its philosophical roots all the way back to the teachings of Plato. The second group represents a child-centered, socially oriented, and humanistic approach based on the works of John Dewey and A.S.Neill. Modern supporters of this second group include Charles Silberman, Edgar Freidenberg, Paul Goodman, John Holt, and Herbert Kohl. One of the teaching strategies supported by this second group is the open school/open classroom approach, which is often associated with the work of Herbert Kohl.

After working with Black sixth graders in East Harlem, Kohl wrote *36 Children* in 1968. In this book, he described a curriculum he created based on his students' experiences and his own imagination. Claiming that he was frustrated by the standard curriculum, which prevented honest communication between students and teachers, Kohl claimed great success with combining creativity and relevant experiences with academic activities. His 1969 book *The Open Classroom: A Practical Guide to a New Way of Teaching* outlined an alternative model for classroom organization, which was used broadly in public schools in the 1970s. In this second book, Kohl described the "battles with self and system" that teachers faced in public schools designed more for controlling students than for teaching them.

While many educators consider open classrooms to be a fad of the 70s, a significant number of educators, including members of the Coalition of Essential Schools, continue to find merit in the progressive concepts and non-authoritarian techniques utilized in open classrooms. There are several open schools in operation with a long-standing record of success, including the Mankato Wilson Campus School, the Jefferson County Open School, and the St. Paul Open School. A recommended resource concerning open classrooms and open schools is Dorothy Fadiman's video "Why Do These Kids Love School?"

Waldorf Schools (Steiner Schools)

Like most Montessori schools, Waldorf schools tend to be private institutions based on the work of a founding individual. In the case of Waldorf schools, the individual is Rudolf Steiner, who developed the concept of anthroposophical (human wisdom) teaching in the early 20th century. The specialized teaching strategies employed in Waldorf or Steiner schools are designed to educate children to "become free, responsible, and active human beings, able to create a just and peaceful society" (Koetzsch). According to the Association of Waldorf Schools of North America's website, the "aim of the education is to fully develop the capacities of each student and to inspire a love for lifelong learning." Waldorf schools are mostly small private institutions organized in a pre-school to twelfth grade format.

Rudolf Steiner founded the first Waldorf School in Stuttgart, Germany in 1919. Today there are eight hundred and eighty schools in fourteen countries; 2003 marks the 75th anniversary of Waldorf education in North America, with over one hundred and forty schools in Canada, Mexico, and the United States.

As is the case with every type of school or educational model, Waldorf or Steiner Schools have both their supporters and critics. For further information about this alternative to public education, access the Association of Waldorf Schools of North America website at http://www.awsna.org/, and for international information, http://www.steinerwaldorf.org.uk/. Information critical of the Waldorf Schools and the Steiner concept may be accessed at http://www.waldorfcritics.org/.

Therapeutic Schools

The term "Therapeutic Schools" is used to describe specialized institutions designed to meet the needs of a variety of troubled young people. According to the National Association of Therapeutic Schools and Programs, these schools "offer programs and professional assistance to young people beleaguered by emotional and behavioral difficulties." Typically residential programs, these schools serve the needs of students unable to thrive in more traditional settings. The exact number of these types of schools is unknown, however, the National Association of Therapeutic Schools and Programs, established in 1999, currently has one hundred and thirteen member schools. An excellent resource for information and listings of therapeutic schools is the National Association of Therapeutic Schools and Programs website: http://www.natsap.org/.

Independent Schools

There are two general terms used to describe the area of non-public schools. They are "private" and " non-public." Most often included in this rather broad category are independent, parochial or religious, Montessori, and for-profit schools. In some ways, the independent schools are distinctly different from other private schools. According to the National Association of Independent Schools, independent schools are unique in that they are independently governed by a board of trustees. In addition, they do not depend on any type of church funding, as is the case with parochial schools, or tax funding, as in the case of public schools.

It is estimated that there are two thousand independent schools operating in the United States, 1,184 of them are members of the National Association of Independent Schools. These member schools enroll over four hundred and eighty-five thousand students with an estimated three hundred thousand additional students attending non-member independent schools. The NAIS believes that there are nearly eight hundred thousand independent school students currently in the United States. For further information concerning independent schools, refer to the NAIS website at http://www.nais.org/.

Private Schools

The term private school is most often used as a catch-all phrase to describe every type of non-public institution. As can be seen from our discussion so far this label is proving to be inadequate. Private school, in the more specific use of the term describes a number of schools developed for specialized purposes. These institutions include college preparatory academies, single-sex schools, special needs schools, military schools, and sports schools. As we will see, there is often a great deal of spillover in terms of school purpose.

College Preparatory Schools, as the name implies, are designed to prepare students for the rigors of higher education. They come in the form of boarding schools, day academies, single gender and co-educational institutions. Some are sponsored through church affiliation while others are non-sectarian enterprises. These schools cater to the needs of students with high academic abilities who often come from higher economic bracket homes.

Single Sex Schools are designed to separate the genders for educational purposes. They are based on the belief that young men and young women experience variations in brain development as well as distinctly different learning styles. Advocates of this type of educational experience believe that both genders profit from a single-sex learning environment. Included in this camp is a group advocating the establishment of gender separate public schools. Further information on this topic can be accessed through the National Association for Single Sex Public Education.

Special Needs Schools are designed to meet the needs of students with disabilities, including vision, hearing, and cognitive challenges. Information concerning these special needs institutions can be accessed through the National Association of Private Schools for Exceptional Children, the National Information Center for Children and Youth with Disabilities, and the Oral Deaf Education Schools.

Military Schools have a long tradition of educating mainly young men. They appeal to students and parents who are seeking a program offering rigorous discipline and solid academic training. While the overall number of military academies declined after World War II, they remain viable options in several parts of the country. Information concerning this type of education can be accessed through the Association of Military Colleges and Schools of the United States.

Sports Schools: While it sometimes seems that the amount of attention given to athletic programs in most public schools would make the establishment of "sports schools" seem redundant, that is apparently not the case. Students seeking a combination of college preparatory academics with a liberal amount of athletic training can find schools that offer specialized coaching in skiing, snowboarding, ice skating, ice hockey, or golf. Further information on these special types of institutions can be found on the web under the heading Sports Schools On-line.

Parochial Schools are defined as schools maintained by a church or religious organization. By far, the greatest number of parochial schools is operated by the Catholic Church. Of the 5,162,684 students who attend private elementary and secondary schools, more than half of them attend Catholic institutions. According to the National Catholic Educational Association, there are currently 6,949 Catholic elementary schools and 1,343 Catholic high schools in operation in this country. Combined with Catholic colleges, universities, and centers for religious education, there are over two hundred thousand Catholic educators serving 7.6 million students.

In America, the largest number of non-Catholic parochial schools is affiliated with the Lutheran Church. Parochial schools have also been established by Quakers, Jews, and other religious groups. Further information concerning Catholic schools may be accessed at the National Catholic Educational Association website: http://www.ncea.org/ and the Catholic Educator's Resource Center: http://catholiceducation.org/.

Clearly private education represents a significant willingness by individuals to fund an alternative form of educational experience for their children. According to the National Center for Educational Statistics, the total enrollment for all elementary and secondary schools is 59.9 million students. Of those 53.2 million attend public school while 6.7 million attend privately funded institutions. Through their taxes, the parents of those 6.7 million students also pay for a public education that they do not access.

Endless Sources

The previous outline of alternatives to the current public school system is in no way meant to be comprehensive. Rather the goal is to demonstrate that there are many alternatives currently being employed by those who are not satisfied with the educational monopoly and are willing to finance alternative schooling on their own. For further information start with the following resources: AERO – The Alternative Education Resource Organization (http://www.edrev.org/links.htm), the website for Path of Learning: An Introduction to Educational Alternatives located at http://www.ratical.org/many_worlds/POL.html, and *The Parent's Guide to Alternatives in Education* by Ronald Koetzsch, Shambhala Press, 1997.

Educational Reform as Opposed to School Reform

In the final analysis most alternative institutions are still essentially schools. While they seek to improve education and avoid the pitfalls of traditional public schools, most alternative settings represent only variations on the old outdated theme. They may be somewhat different in their structure or organization, but many are still essentially inefficient.

Most of the attempts at school reform in past years would be the stuff of high comedy if the results were not so tragic. Some schools have tried to ease the pressure of the evaluation process by issuing 1s, 2s, and 3s instead of A through F grades, fooling absolutely no one. Other schools have instituted block schedules in which students endure ninety minutes of material that seems irrelevant rather than a mere fifty-five minutes. Like public schools, some alternative schools emphasize working on students' self-esteem so that they can feel better about themselves while remaining academically inept. In some cases, school personnel encourage students to chant, "I am somebody," without ever admonishing them to "do something." Many schools spend more energy on political correctness than they do on political science. Still others evaluate students on the basis of "how hard they try" rather than on what they accomplish. Most schools attempt to celebrate diversity without ever lamenting ineptitude. Yet others expend energy establishing programs to develop assertive discipline rather than demanding an acceptable level of deportment, and permanently deporting those who refuse to behave.

True progress will not occur until we fully realize that during this last century the institution we call "school" has become, in effect, the "alternative" to education. The authors firmly believe that it need not be this way. True educational freedom will result in the demise of traditionally funded schools. The first step is ending the monopoly by busting the public school trust. The second is convincing people that modern, effective, education has very little to do with what we historically think of as schools.

Of Transportation Kings and Education Presidents

While it is true that we are in the midst of yet another futile round of educational reform, we believe that this effort like so many others is an example of administrative whirling disease. *No Child Left Behind* is the latest in a long series of politically mandated, educational versions of St. Vitas Dance.

These endless cycles of American educational reform are, in many ways, reminiscent of the old story of the medieval kingdom where all of the ox carts and wagons had square wheels. With every rotation of the wheels the cart went clunk, clunk, clunk, clunk and the passengers held on for dear life. Being aware of the situation and sensitive to the needs of his subjects, the king ordered his best engineers to quickly address the problem.

After weeks of deliberation and political wrangling, the panel of engineers announced that the problem had been solved. With great fan-fare and ceremony, they unveiled the new and improved three-sided wagon wheel. Three sides, they proudly explained, offered a 25 percent improvement over the old four-sided wheel and only went chunk, clunk, clunk with each rotation. The king congratulated the committee on improving transportation by a factor of 25 percent and renamed himself the Transportation King. The riders in the carts and wagons continued to hang on for dear life.

Our seemingly endless cycles of reform, supported by a never-ending supply of "education presidents" and "education governors," consist of dialogue, discussion, fanfare, and woefully little substance. Challenges are issued, committees are formed, policies are changed, reports are written, money is spent, and success is declared. Students and teachers throughout a century of endless reform have tenaciously hung on to the same bouncing cart, realizing that little or nothing has ever changed. Without question, the time for real change is at hand. It is time to leave school and find education.

How Cold Is It?

Bostonians listening to the popular radio station WBZ as they commute to work are dependent upon news anchor Gary LaPierre for the weather report. Known as the Walter Cronkite of New England, LaPierre leads his listeners to believe he is freezing in the snow with them when the mercury hits six degrees.

It turns out that LaPierre has been anchoring the show from St. Augustine, Florida, for the past 2 years where the mercury rarely dips below 40 degrees in the winter.

Station manager Ted Jordan doesn't think it's such a big deal. Asked if he thought it was unethical for the weatherman to exclaim, "Would you believe it's 5 below 0 now," from St. Augustine, Jordan said "no." Not being physically present when reporting is not that unusual, the station manager explained.

Source: Boston Globe, January 15, 2004.

Twelve Conclusions

The fact that you have stayed with us through seven chapters indicates that you have some serious concerns about the state of education in America. Through these chapters we believe that we have established the following points.

1. There are profound differences between the educational demands of the 21st century and the antiquated services that schools are capable of providing.

2. A growing number of American parents are finding the core activities and values presented in schools to be inconsistent with the educational needs that they identify for their children.

3. During the last century, the potential and capabilities of learning technologies have grown exponentially, while the development of school-based practices have remained essentially static.

4. Through the course of the 20th century, nearly every major competitive enterprise has been forced to adapt to change or perish, while schools have been enabled to maintain a consistent monopoly on educational funding.

5. Despite the exponential technological and social changes evident during the last century, perennial supporters of the traditional school model have enthusiastically advocated a return to antiquated curricular models that are pre-medieval in their design and function.

6. The concept of mandatory universal education for individuals who obviously don't want to learn, and are willing and able to disrupt the process for those who do, is clearly outdated.

7. The most significant movements toward school reform have been orchestrated by politicians, whose motives are suspect and whose knowledge of education is clearly lacking.

8. In a functional democracy, citizens should never be forced to do business with clearly dysfunctional monopolies.

9. Despite more than a century of warnings by experts in the field, schools have consistently avoided significant change processes and only attempted reform efforts that amount to symbolic tinkering.

10. With the advent of the Internet and computer technology, education abruptly ceased being a place-bound limited process carried out in schools and became a lifelong endeavor to be enjoyed and practiced any where, at any time.

11. Leaving schools will return education to its pre-20th century format of accessing learning opportunities through a variety of sources in modes that can be tailored to individual learner's needs.

12. There is a world of difference between school reform and educational reform. It is now obvious that school reform is both hopeless and pointless. Educational reform is essential!

The question remains, "Can I do anything as an individual to expedite this process?" The answer is, resoundingly, "Yes!" We believe that the willingness of California voters to recall their newly elected governor is an indicator of American citizens' growing determination to become much more actively involved in directing their own futures. The same type of hands-on approach will have a dramatic effect in changing the nature of American education.

Postscript

The arguments outlined in this book will remain just that until tested. It will take initiatives by groups and individuals to move our public schools off-center and to open the doors for finding true education. To those interested in such a quest, we would make the following observation: the two forces that historically have moved public education are law and money.

The law provides a very promising avenue for those wishing to reform education in America. The fact that the Massachusetts Assembly in 1650 mandated taxes to support school, or that the Michigan Supreme Court upheld taxation for secondary schools in 1874 does not mean that taxation for education is legal. The U.S. Supreme Court has never reviewed this topic of taxation for public education, and there are some promising reasons why this practice of taxation might be overturned.

At the heart of any such argument lies in the Tenth Amendment to the United States Constitution, which states, "The powers not delegated to the United States by the Constitution, nor prohibited by it to the states, are reserved to the states respectively, *or to the people.*" When broken down, a legal interpretation would hold that issues (powers) not specifically assigned to the United States (not delegated) remain under the authority of each individual state, *or to the people* of each state.

In one interpretation of this phraseology, a free nation is made up of free states, and controlled by free people – who are free to make their own choices. This choosing is made even more interesting by the wording of the Fourteenth Amendment of the U.S. Constitution, Section 1, that reads "No state shall make or enforce any law which shall abridge the privileges or immunities of the citizens of the United States, nor shall any State deprive any person of life, liberty, *or property* without due process of law. If the reader has ever wondered why the federal government leaves Quakers alone in terms of school attendance, Mormons alone on the question of multiple wives, and remains fairly passive in the prosecution of tax evaders, this may be a clue. Many individuals have questioned the intended meaning of *or to the people.* There are even organized bodies, such as the Kansas Tenth Amendment Society, seeking to clarify these promises of our founding fathers.

Certainly, it would not take an amendment of the U.S. Constitution to get the ball rolling to help parents regain control of our schools. Any state wishing to challenge existing funding patterns or the control of funding for public (and private) education could use a state constitutional amendment to clarify the issues. Once the signatures are collected and the issue is placed on the ballot, there is a very good chance that it would pass. The best possibilities would be in states in the south and far west where funding pressures are the greatest and the satisfaction with schools is the lowest.

The second major force in bringing about educational reform is money. Money to schools is like gasoline to cars. When money is present, schools move forward. At the time of this writing, billions of dollars are "locked up" in schools. Just to use a small example, 1.7 million students are now home schooling, but the schools have retained the money earmarked for the education of each pupil. To pry loose the $7,000-8,000 per student for use in alternative initiatives would start a small stampede of demand for "choice" by parents.

All of this, of course, takes us to the voucher issue, which has been explored in this book. The importance of this issue grows daily. In Florida, for instance, the state government has taken public funds for education and has given twenty-four thousand students tuition vouchers for private schools. The authors believe that the "failing schools" strategy being used by Governor Jeb Bush to accomplish this transfer of funds to private schools has severe limitations. A much more attractive strategy for those who care about education in this country would be to allow students on the "high end" academically to use their allocation to purchase education services in the open market (including electronic delivery of Internet portals). In the case of Florida, the twenty-four thousand students represent $168 million – enough to launch an electronic education industry. Again, the power of voters in any state can make this happen through constitutional amendment.

In conclusion, the authors believe we are poised, unknowingly, on the brink of a major change in education in the United States. Our schools, while imposing in scale, are precariously fragile in reality. Any coalition of parents, taxpayers, businessmen, and concerned educators has the power to influence the most significant change in American education. The question is, "What are we waiting for?"

Appendix
Prototype Learning Portal – 2004

Education and Training Sites

College Degrees

Online Guide to Universities Offering Degrees (University of Illinois, Phoenix, DeVry, St. Leo) – Bachelors, masters, doctoral levels. www.classeusa.com/featuredschools/

Bachelors Degree – North Central Association accredited program. Capella Univeristy. Degrees in business, technology, education, human services, psychology. www.capella.com

Masters Degree – Regents University, Virginia Beach, VA, full masters online. Four-month residence to complete. www.regents.edu

Masters Degree – Online anytime instruction. Class interaction, questions answered, four semesters. University of Colorado, Colorado Springs. http://business.uccs.edu/information/

K-12

GED Online – Assessments, worksheets. Graduate high school at home. www.gedonlineclass.com/class_info/index.htm

GED Prep Class – www.ged-secrets.com

SAT Prep – Verbal section only. www.teracomps.com/

Physics Tutors – Remedial and advanced tutoring in physics. www.physics.uoguelph.ca/tutorials/tutorials.htm

Seminars Online – Various topics in art, history, culture, science, technology at the Smithsonian. www.si.edu

Learning Partners – Geography, history, math, science, etc. Help with homework, writing papers, library use. www.ed.gov/pubs/parents/learnPtours/

Library Tutorial – Learn how to use a library from Bowling Green State University. www.bgsu.edu/

<u>Dictionaries and Such</u> – Merriam-Webster online. Oxford English Dictionary and others. www.w-m.com

<u>Talking Library</u> – Twenty-two thousand sites in art, social studies, math, science, English, health and PE, foreign language. Browse in multiple languages. Some guidance and counseling. www.awesomelibrary.org

<u>Journals Online</u> – Links to education and medical journals online (thirty-five different sources). www.lesley.edu/faculty/kholmes/libguides/edjounals.html

<u>Academic Tutoring</u> – All subjects in English. Free download software. www.avant-gardeglobalonlinetutoring.cn/

K-12 Subjects (example: Math)

A complete content curriculum for mathematics K-12. http://mathforum.org/mathtools

Math lesson plans, all levels. http://www.mathsearch.com/arithmatic

North Carolina public schools curriculum for math. http://www.ncpublicschools.rog/curriculum/mathematics

Performance objectives for mathematics K-12. http://www.coe.west.asu.edu/students/Westwind

Worksheets, puzzles, test prep for math – all levels. http://www.edhelper.com/math.htm

Math questions? Ask the experts. Email contact with professors. http://www.mathforum.org/dr.math

Helping girls in math-assessment, tutoring, grades 3-12. http://www.colormathpink.com

Self-scoring math practice problems. http://www.mathmastery.com

Learning/Others

<u>Language Instruction for Children</u> – www.early-advantage.com/about_Muzzy/

<u>Learn Islamic</u> – www.nitle.org/arabworld/links.php

Spanish Grammar Tutorial – Parts of speech, gender of nouns, adjectives, nouns, etc. www.studyspanish.com/tutorials

Ballroom Dancing – Teaches a variety of ballroom dance steps. www.dancetv.com/tutorial

Language Translator – Thirteen olanguages to any of the other twelve. Type n' click. http://babelfish.altavista.com/babelfish/tr

Reading Music – Clefs, time signatures, notes. www.datadragon.com

Children's Music Helper – Learn to compose and play music online. http://creativemusic.com

Flight Simulator – Take-off, touch and go landings, radio navigation. www.firstflight.com/lessons/syl/htm

Information Sources

News to the Moment – Top stories. www.cnn.com

World Newspapers – In English, all regions of the world, one hundred countries. www.world-newspapers.com

New York Times – Online, abbreviated free paper. Thirty-day story search. www.nytimes.com

News, News, News – Twenty-five leading newspapers (Chicago Tribune, USA Today) from U.S. http://school.discovery.com/homeworkhelper

World Museum Guide – By topic and by museum. Smithsonian, Louvre, British Museum, Field Museum of Natural History. www.museumstuff.com

Metropolitan Museum of Art – Question and answer capability. www.metmuseum.org/visitor/faq_hist.htm

Jobfinder – Employment ads, resume posting. www.wholelottajobs.com

Career Counseling – Testing, advice, counseling. www.mylifecoach.com

Federal Job Search – Thousands of jobs in the database accessed by location, salary, etc. www.federaljobsearch.com/default.asp

Buying and Selling Stuff – www.ebay.com

Health Assessment – Quizzes from mental health to allergies.
www.mayoclinic.com

Baby News – Development, pregnancy, products, nutrition.
www.babycenter.com

Make Surveys – Design, collect responses, analyze using the survey maker.
www.surveymonkey.com

Word Lyrics – Remember the words to your favorite song?
http://lyrics.astraweb.com

Your House from Space – Satellite view of your town, neighborhood, and
even your house form outer space. www.terraserver.com

Occupational Titles – Alphabetized dictionary with description of work done.
www.occupationalinfo.org

Old Faithful – picture taken every twenty-nine seconds from webcam at Old
Faithful. www.nps.gov/yell/oldfaithfulcam.htm

Music Archives – Fifty databases for primarily classical music. Locate and
listen. www2.siba.fi/kulttuuripalvelut/libraries.html

Musical Instrument Museum – Ten thousand instruments from the beginning
of history. www.usd.edu/music

Self Assessment and Development

Personality Test – IQ, health screen, career tests, self-scoring.
www.daviddeck.com

Personality Assessment – Career values, Keirsey Temperament Sorter,
Colors test, Lifestyles. www.2h.com/personality-tests.htm

Myers-Briggs – Personality typing using the Myers-Briggs Type Indicator.
www.myerbrigggs.org/

Cognitive Style – Learning style assessment by Boise State.
www.coenboisestate.edu/dep/ipt/lsa.htm

Jung Typology Test – Personality inventory. www.humanmetrics.com

Intelligence Type – Using Gardiner's eight intelligences. Assess your strengths. http://emints.more.net/ethenes/resources/S00000718.html

MENSA Workout – Brainy questions to see how you match up with the bright ones. www.mensa.org/workout.html

Interactive IQ Test – measures cognitive performance, word analysis, spatial reasoning. www.funeducation.com/products/iqtest

IQ Test – Math, verbal, spatial, reasoning, short-term memory assessments. www.intelligencetest.com

Nutrition Analysis – Do you eat right? Energy calculator. www.ag.uiuc.edu/~food-lb/nut/

Women's Health – Eating disorders, heart disease, body image, pregnancy. www.4women.gov/

Workout for Women – Online training, weight loss, newsletter, workout log. www.workoutsforwomen.com/default.asp

Weight Watchers – Online programs at your fingertips. Twelve-day introductory newsletter-points calculator. www.weightwatchers.com

Leisure and Entertainment

Fitness – Workouts for children. www.fitnessonline.com

Virtual Golf – 3-D graphics, compete with other players, virtual caddie assistance. www.microsoft.com/sports/golf/whats_new.htm

Exercise – Improve muscle strength, aerobic exercise, heart rate calculation, simulated stretching exercise. www.lifeclinic.com/focus/nutrition

Workout – With the U.S. Army at Fort Benning. Pictures of repetitions. www.benning.army.mil/usapfs/Training

Walking Consultant – Tips for losing weight. Responds to email. www.diynet.com

Virtual Vacations – Children introduce you to three hundred wonderful places. www.scms.osceola.k12.fl.us/cool/vacations/list/html

Gardening – How to plant, prep soil, mulch, prune.
www.bathgardencenter.com

Butterfly Garden – How to prepare. Beautiful pictures.
www.uky.edu/agriculture/entomology/entfacts/misc/

Photography – Twenty lessons in taking pictures by Kodak. www.kodak.com

Lawn and Landscaping – Do it yourself series. www.diynet.com

Irrigation Systems – Design and install your own system.
www.class.universalclass.com

Guitar Lessons – Online playing lessons plus theory and repair tips.
www.personal.psu.edu

Learn to Sew – For beginners. Step-by-step instruction. Pictures.
www.sewnews.com/es/beginners

Learn to Write – Online instruction for poets, novels, screenwriters.
www.writers.com

Suggestions for Reading – Topical. New books. Reviews.
www.Amazon.com

Volunteer at the Zoo – Be an intern at the San Diego Zoo. Eight weeks of
virtual volunteering. Behind the scenes. www.kn.pacbell.com/wired/

Go on an Artic Expedition – Virtual interaction with expedition in Alaska.
www.arcus.org/articalive/expeditions.html

Be an Artist – Learn to paint, arrange flowers, paint tiles.
www.handpaintedtiles.com/be-an-artist.htm

Home Repairs – Do it yourself tutorial. www.homedepot.com

Citations and Readings

Adler, M. 1982. *Paideia Proposal.* New York: Macmillan.

Barker, J. A. 1992. *Future Edge*: *Discovering the New Paradigms of Success.* New York: William Morrow and Co., Inc.

Bobbitt, F. 1913. *The Supervision of City Schools: Twelfth Yearbook of the National Society for the Study of Education, Part I.* Chicago: University of Chicago Press.

Boulding, K. E. 1964. *The Meaning of the Twentieth Century: The Great Transition.* New York: Harper and Row.

Boyer, E. 1983. *High School: A Report on Secondary Education in America.* New York: Harper and Row.

Bruner, J. 1960. *The Process of Education.* New York: Macmillan.

Commission on Excellence, The. 1983. *A Nation at Risk.*

Counts, G. S. 1932. *Dare the School Build a New Social Order?* New York: John Day.

Covey, S. R. 1989. *The Seven Habits of Highly Effective People.* New York: Simon and Schuster, Inc.

Cubberly, E. P. 1909. *Changing Conceptions of Education.* Boston: Houghton Mifflin.

Cubberly, E. P. 1920. *The History of Education.* Boston: Houghton Mifflin.

Drucker, P. F. 1974. *Management: Tasks, Practices, Responsibilities.* New York: Harper and Row.

Eliot, C. W. 1892. *Wherein Popular Education Has Failed.* The Forum.

Federal Population Census. 1900. Washington, D.C.: U.S. National Archives and Records Administration.

Frady, M. 1985. *To Save Our Schools, To Save Our Children.* Far Hills, NJ: New Horizon Press.

Gallup, A. 1984. The Gallup Poll of Teacher's Attitudes Toward the Public Schools. *Phi Delta Kappan* 66 (October).

Greenhoe, F. 1941. *Community Contacts and Participation of Teachers*, Washington, D.C.: American Council on Public Affairs.

Hall, G. S. 1905. *Adolescence*. Vol. 1. New York: D. Appleton Century.

Harris, L., Libresco, J. D., and Parker, R. P. 1984. *The American Teacher*. New York: The Metropolitan Life Insurance Company.

Hazards Register of Pennsylvania. 1835. Vol. 15, No. 18, 2 May.

Holt, J. 1964. *How Children Fail*. New York: Dell Publishing Co.

Illich, I. 1972. *De-schooling Society*. New York: Harper and Row.

Illich, I. 1973. *After Schooling What?* New York: Perennial Library.

Johns, R. L., Morphet, E. L., and Alexander, K. 1982. *The Economics and Financing of Education*. 4th ed. Upper Saddle River, NJ: Prentice-Hall, Inc.

Kozol, J. 1991. *Savage Inequalities: Children in America's Schools*. New York: Harper Perennial.

Llewellyn, G. 1991. *Teenage Liberation Handbook: How to Quit School and Get a Real Life and Education*. Eugene, OR: Lowery House.

Lortie, D. C. 1975. *School Teacher: A Sociological Study*. Chicago: University of Chicago Press.

McLuhan, M. 1964. Automation: Learning a Living. In *Understanding Media*. New York: McGraw-Hill.

McLuhan, M. and Fiore, Q. 1967. *The Medium is the Message*. New York: Bantam Books.

Mort, P. R. and Vincent, W. S. 1946. *A Look at Our Schools: A Book for the Thinking Citizen*. New York: Cattell.

National Education Association. 1893. *Committee of Ten on Secondary School Studies*. Washington, D.C.: U.S. Printing Office.

National Education Association. 1895. Committee of Fifteen Report. In *Address and Proceedings*. Washington, D.C.: NEA.

National Education Association. 1987. *Status of the American Public School Teacher: 1985-1986*. Washington, D.C.: NEA.

National Center for Educational Statistics. 1986. *Statistics of State School Systems and Center for Educational Statistics*. Washington, D.C.: U.S. Department of Education.

National Center for Educational Statistics. 1997. *Job Satisfaction Among America's Teachers: Effects of Workplace Conditions, Background Characteristics, and Teacher Compensation, July 1997*. Washington, D.C.: U.S. Department of Education, Office of Educational Research and Improvement.

National Center for Educational Statistics. 2001. *Digest of Educational Statistics*. Retrieved from http://nces.ed.gov//pubs2002.

Ogburn, W. F. 1966. *Social Change*. New York: Dell Publishing Co.

Parker, F. W. 1894. *Talks on Pedagogics*. New York: E.L. Kellogg.

Palmer, P. 1998. *The Courage to Teach*. San Francisco: Jossey Bass.

Peckman, J. A. 1977. *Federal Tax Policy*. 3rd ed. Washington, D.C.: Brookings Institution.

Perelman, L. J. 1992. *School's Out*. New York: Avon Books.

Platt, J. 1966. *The Step to Man*. New York: John Wiley.

Popular Electronics Magazine. 1975. Exclusive Article. (January).

Pulliam, J. D. 1987. *History of Education in America*. 4th ed. Columbus, OH: Merrill Publishing Co.

Readers Digest Association. 1975. *Family Encyclopedia of American History*. Vol. 1. Pleasantville, NY: Author.

Senge, P. M. and Drucker, P.F. 2001. *Leading in a Time of Change*. Video Conversation With Peter Drucker and Peter Senge. New York: The Drucker Foundation.

Shannon, J. 1973. The Property Tax: Reform or Relief? In *Property Tax Reform,* Edited by G. E. Peterson. Washington D.C.: Urban Institute.

Steed, Tom. 1967. Tom Steed speaking at congressional hearing. *History of the U.S. Postal Service.* Retrieved from http://www.usps.com/history/his3.htm#reform

Steven, Thaddeus. 1835. Thaddeus Steven address to the Pennsylvania House of Representatives. *Register of Pennsylvania,* 2 May, Vol. 15, No. 18.

Teacher Education Reports. 1985. Vol. 7. (September 26).

Toffler, A. 1970. *Future Shock.* New York: Random House.

Tye, B. and O'Brien, L. 2002. Why are Experienced Teachers Leaving the Profession. *Phi Delta Kappan,* September, 24-32.

U.S. Congress Office of Technology Assessment. 1988. *Power On! New Tools for Teaching and Learning.* Washington DC: GPO.

U.S. Surgeon General Vaughn. 1918. Influenza. *American Experience.* Retrieved from http://www.pbs.org/wgbh/amex/influenza/filmore/description.html

Walberg, H. 1970. Professional Role Discontinuities in Educational Careers. *Review of Educational Research* 40 (June).

Webb, R. B. and Sherman, R. R. 1989. *Schooling and Society.* New York: Macmillan Publishing Co.

Luminaries

Schools are the slaughterhouses of the mind. – John Amos Cominus

School methodologies – childhood with its beauty gone and only its helplessness remaining. – Charles Dickens

When in the year 2000 the historian writes his account of the period through which we are now passing, he will see us in this strange fantastic industrial society repeating formula handed down from an agrarian age when we should be searching with tireless effort for formula suited to the world as it is. – George Counts

It is customary for adults to forget how hard and dull and long school is. – John Steinbeck

Continued in their present pattern of fragmented unrelation, our school curricula will insure a citizenry unable to understand the cybernated world in which they live. – Marshall McLuhan

The weakness of American education is that it educates to the wrong ends ... it simply never occurs to more than a handful to ask why we are doing what we are doing ... to think seriously or deeply about the consequences of education. – Charles Silberman

The fact that education chooses to continually overlook is that today we have the technology to enable virtually anyone to learn anything, anywhere, anytime, with excellent results. – Lewis Perleman

The aim of school is simply to reduce as many individuals as possible to the same safe level, to breed and train a standardized citizenry, to put down dissent and originality. – H. L. Mencken

By focusing on schools and teachers in schools, planners are forced to operate within the parameters of the institution ... this tends to filter out all ideas which might improve education. – Bruce Joyce

Notes

Notes